WRITERS AND THEIR WORK

ISOBEL ARMSTRONG
General Editor

KT-212-692

ATHOL FUGARD

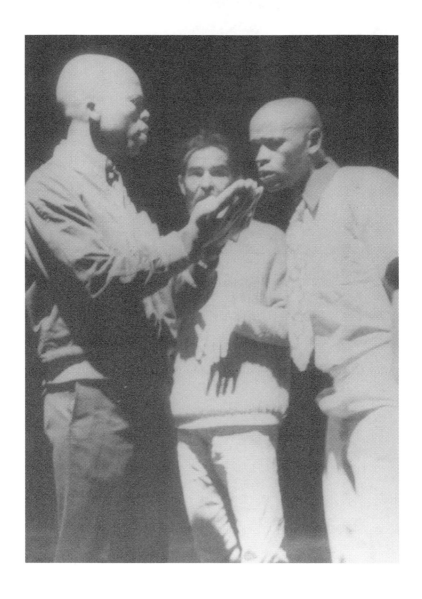

John Kani and Winston Ntshona, directed by Athol Fugard in the 1973
Royal Court rehearsal of *Sizwe Bansi*. Photograph by courtesy of the
National English Literary Museum, Grahamstown, South Africa.

ATHOL FUGARD

Dennis Walder

Northcote House
in association with the
British Council

© Copyright 2003 by Dennis Walder

First published in 2003 by Northcote House Publishers Ltd, Horndon, Tavistock, Devon, PL19 9NQ, United Kingdom.
Tel: +44 (01822) 810066. Fax: +44 (01822) 810034.

British Library Cataloguing-in-Publication Data
A catalogue record for this book is available from the British Library

ISBN 0-7463-1021-8 hb
ISBN 0-7463-0948-1 pb

Typeset by TW Typesetting, Plymouth, Devon
Printed and bound in the United Kingdom by Athenaeum Press Ltd.

For Anna

Contents

Acknowledgements

I am grateful to Marcia Blumberg (Toronto), Miki Flockemann (Cape Town) and Robert Fraser (London) for reading and commenting upon my final draft, and to Ann Torlesse, Chief Curator of the National English Literary Museum, Grahamstown, South Africa, for her assistance in obtaining material. Athol Fugard himself has always been generous in responding to requests – for information, interviews and, specifically for my purposes in this book, a pre-publication copy of *Sorrows and Rejoicings*.

Biographical Outline

1932 11 June: Harold Athol Lanigan Fugard born in Middelburg, Cape Province, South Africa, to Harold David Lanigan Fugard and Elizabeth Magdalena, née Potgieter.

1935 Fugard family, including older brother Royal and younger sister Glenda, moves to Port Elizabeth, on the Eastern Cape coast.

1938–45 Fugard (known as Hally) attends Marist Brothers College, Port Elizabeth. Parents run Jubilee Residential Hotel, then, from 1941, Mrs Fugard takes over the St George's Park Tearoom in the city centre. Difficult times, made harder by father's invalidism.

1946–50 Port Elizabeth Technical College on a council bursary. Studies motor mechanics and acts in school play.

1950–2 Studies for BA at University of Cape Town, majoring in Philosophy, with Social Science, Anthropology, French. Drafts a novel, which he destroys, and writes poetry.

1953 June: sets off before final exams with Perseus Adams to hitch-hike up Africa. Leaves Adams in Sudan and enrols as 'captain's tiger' on British tramp-steamer. Throws second attempt at novel overboard.

1954 Returns to Port Elizabeth after round-the-world voyage. Writing freelance for *Evening Post*.

1955–7 Joins South African Broadcasting Corporation as regional news reporter, transferred to Cape Town. 22 September 1956: marries actress Sheila Meiring.

They establish the Circle Players, who perform his *Klaas and the Devil*, and *The Cell*, now lost.

1958   Clerk in the Fordsburg Native Commissioner's Court, Johannesburg, a formative experience. 30 August: *No-Good Friday*, premiere, Bantu Men's Social Centre, Johannesburg. Stage manager and pre-publicity agent for National Theatre Organization. Dr H. F. Verwoerd becomes Prime Minister. Treason Trial continues.

1959   8 June: *Nongogo*, premiere, Bantu Men's Social Centre, Johannesburg, then Darragh Hall, Johannesburg.

1960   London: turned down by Royal Court. With Sheila, joins Tone Brulin in the New Africa Group, which performs prize-winning try-for-white play, *A Kakamas Greek*, with Fugard, at Festival of Avantgarde Theatre, Brussels. 21 March: Sharpeville massacre and five-month State of Emergency in South Africa, to which they return. Works on *Tsotsi*, *The Blood Knot* and begins notebooks.

1961   27 May: birth of daughter, Lisa Maria. 3 September: *The Blood Knot* performed with Zakes Mokae at Dorkay House, Johannesburg. Reduced version tours for six months. South Africa becomes a republic, after expulsion from the British Commonwealth.

1962   Open letter to British playwrights leads to boycott of performances of their plays in segregated venues.

1963   *The Blood Knot* at the New Arts Theatre, Hampstead, London, with Ian Bannen and Zakes Mokae, dir. John Berry. Begins association with the Serpent Players, directing adaptations of Machiavelli, Camus, Brecht, Beckett, Sophocles. Purchases house at Schoenmakerskop, outside Port Elizabeth.

1964   *The Blood Knot* at the Cricket Theatre, New York, with James Earl Jones and J. D. Cannon.

1965   First improvisations with the Serpent Players. 26 October: *Hello and Goodbye* opens at the Library Theatre, Johannesburg, with Fugard and Molly Seftel, dir. Barney Simon. Several Serpent Players arrested.

1966   Forms short-lived Ijinle Company, Hampstead The-
        atre Club, to perform *The Blood Knot* and Soyinka's
        Trials of Brother Jero. The Coat performed in Port
        Elizabeth. Dr Verwoerd assassinated, succeeded by
        B. J. Vorster.

1967   *The Blood Knot* produced for BBC TV; the day after
        transmission, Fugard's passport withdrawn.

1968   First appearances of John Kani and Winston
        Ntshona on stage. 13 March: *People Are Living There*,
        premiere, Close Theatre, Glasgow. *Mille Miglia* ap-
        pears on BBC TV. Prohibition of Political Interfer-
        ence Act: extinction of Liberal Party.

1969   14 June: *People Are Living There*, Cape Town, with
        Fugard and Yvonne Bryceland. 10 July: *Boesman
        and Lena*, premiere, Rhodes University Theatre,
        Grahamstown.

1970   *Boesman and Lena* tours; New York premiere with
        James Earl Jones, Ruby Dee and Zakes Mokae.

1971   24 March: *Orestes*, Castlemarine Auditorium, Cape
        Town. Fugard's passport returned after public peti-
        tion, to enable him to direct *Boesman and Lena* at the
        Royal Court Theatre Upstairs in London, with Zakes
        Mokae, Yvonne Bryceland and Bloke Modisane.

1972   28 March: *Statements after an Arrest under the Im-
        morality Act* opens at The Space Theatre, Cape
        Town, with Fugard and Bryceland, followed on 8
        October by *Sizwe Banzi* [sic] *Is Dead* devised with
        and performed by Kani and Ntshona. (This original
        spelling was altered to *Sizwe Bansi* for subsequent
        performances.)

1973   2 July: *The Island*, also in collaboration with Kani and
        Ntshona, premieres as *Die Hodoshe Span*, The Space
        Theatre. *Boesman and Lena* filmed by Ross Devenish,
        with Fugard and Bryceland. Purchases house in
        Nieuw Bethesda. MS of *The Blood Knot* deposited at
        the National English Literary Museum, Grahams-
        town, thereafter main depository of Fugard's pa-
        pers. From 12 December: 'South African Season'
        (including *Sizwe Bansi* and *The Island*) at the Royal
        Court.

1974   From 22 January: *Statements* joins *Sizwe Bansi* and *The Island* at the Royal Court. *Sizwe Bansi* and *The Island* transfer to New York. Fugard changes view on playwrights' boycott. *No-Good Friday* and *Nongogo* at Crucible Theatre, Sheffield. Builds house at Sardinia Bay, 'The Ashram'.

1975   27 August: *Dimetos*, commissioned by Edinburgh Festival, premiere, Church Hill Theatre.

1976   Revised productions of *Dimetos*, Nottingham and London. *Boesman and Lena* opens in Paris in French. 16 June, Soweto Rising. Market Theatre, Johannesburg, opens.

1977   Film of *The Guest at Steenkampskraal* premiered BBC2 on 5 March, subsequently as *The Guest* on 13 September, starring Fugard, who also appears in Peter Brook's film *Meetings with Remarkable Men*. Screenplay of *The Guest* published. *Hello and Goodbye* filmed by South African Broadcasting Corporation. Steve Biko dies in detention. Black Consciousness movements banned.

1978   30 November: *A Lesson from Aloes*, premiere, Market Theatre, with Marius Weyers, Shelagh Holliday and Fugard as Steve Daniel. P. W. Botha succeeds Vorster and launches 'total onslaught' against enemies of apartheid.

1979   Ross Devenish documentary on *A Lesson from Aloes* for BBC TV. South African theatres desegregated.

1980   Six-month fellowship at Yale, editing Notebooks (with Mary Benson) and directing *Aloes* for Yale Rep, leading to further try-outs there later. *The Drummer*, Actors' Theatre Festival, Louisville, Kentucky. *Marigolds in August* (film: dir. Ross Devenish) released. *Tsotsi* published.

1981   Plays General Smuts in Richard Attenborough's film *Gandhi*. Honorary Doctorate, University of Natal. From 23 December: *Dimetos*, The People's Space, Cape Town. *Sizwe Bansi* filmed by CBS Cable.

1982   12 March: *'Master Harold' . . . and the Boys*, premiere, Yale Repertory Theatre, New Haven. Banned in South Africa, ban set aside on appeal. Subsequently at the Market, and the National, London, a pattern followed throughout the 1980s. *Fugard's People*, documentary by Helena Noguiera, premiere, Johannesburg Film Festival, later shown on BBC TV.

1983   *Notebooks: 1960–77* published. Honorary Doctorate, Rhodes University. *Evening Standard* Drama Award for *'Master Harold' . . . and the Boys*.

1984   1 May: *The Road to Mecca*, premiere, Yale Repertory Theatre. Commonwealth Theatre Award, more Honorary Doctorates, including Yale University. Stars in *The Killing Fields*. Lorimer Productions' film of *'Master Harold'* released. Fugard admits earlier alcohol addiction.

1985   State of Emergency in South Africa. AA Life Vita Award for *The Road to Mecca*. 25th Anniversary production of *Blood Knot* (revised title, to reflect substantially revised text), Yale Repertory Theatre.

1986   Repeal of several apartheid laws, including Immorality Act and Pass laws.

1987   24 March: *A Place with the Pigs*, premiere, Yale Repertory Theatre. Civil unrest in South Africa continues.

1989   27 June: *My Children! My Africa!*, premiere, Market Theatre. Lisa Fugard appears in New York production. *Time* magazine calls Fugard 'the greatest active playwright in the English-speaking world'. F. W. De Klerk succeeds Botha as President.

1990   Unbanning of liberation movements; release of Nelson Mandela; Emergency revoked; repeal of remaining apartheid legislation. Fugard awarded Honorary Doctorate, Witwatersrand University.

1991   Release of Peter Goldsmid film of *The Road to Mecca*, with Yvonne Bryceland, Kathy Bates and Fugard. Civil unrest.

1992   16 July: *Playland*, premiere, Market Theatre, with John Kani and Sean Taylor. US try-outs include La Jolla Playhouse production in San Diego, an important venue since 1990 for US performances of his work.

1993   *Playland* at Manhattan Theatre Club with Kevin Spacey and Frankie Faison.

1994 27–30 April: first fully democratic elections; Mandela becomes President. 9 July: *My Life*, premiere, National Arts Festival, Grahamstown. Publication of *Cousins*, first part of memoir. South Africa rejoins British Commonwealth.

1995 15 August: *Valley Song*, premiere, Market Theatre, with Fugard and Esmeralda Biehl, followed by US premiere, McCarter Theatre, Princeton, in October, with Lisa Gay Hamilton replacing Biehl.

1996 31 January: *Valley Song*, UK premiere, Royal Court, with Fugard and Biehl.

1997 5 August: *The Captain's Tiger*, premiere, The Arena, State Theatre, Pretoria, with Fugard, Owen Sejake and Betty Steyn.

1998 8 May: *The Captain's Tiger*, US premiere, McCarter Theatre, Princeton, co-directed by Susan Hilferty, longstanding Fugard collaborator.

1999 Acquisition of Fugard papers by Lilly Library, Indiana University.

2000 18 October: *The Captain's Tiger*, UK premiere, Orange Tree Theatre, Richmond (London), with two actors playing Fugard role. Fugard sells 'The Ashram' and moves semi-permanently to environs of San Diego.

2001 4 May: *Sorrows and Rejoicings*, premiere, McCarter Theatre, Princeton, followed by New York and Cape Town productions.

Abbreviations and References

C.   *Cousins: A Memoir* (Johannesburg: Witwatersrand University Press, 1994)

CT   *The Captain's Tiger* (Johannesburg: Witwatersrand University Press, 1997)

IP   *Interior Plays*, preface by Athol Fugard, ed. and intro. Dennis Walder (Oxford: Oxford University Press, 2000); comprises *People Are Living There, Statements after an Arrest under the Immorality Act, Dimetos, The Guest* (screenplay), *A Lesson from Aloes*

MM   *My Children! My Africa!* (London: Faber & Faber, 1990)

N.   *Notebooks: 1960–1977*, ed. Mary Benson (London: Faber & Faber, 1983)

P.   *Playland . . . and Other Words* (Johannesburg: Witwatersrand University Press, 1992)

PEP   *Port Elizabeth Plays*, ed. and intro. Dennis Walder, with a new preface by Athol Fugard (Oxford: Oxford University Press, 2000), comprises *'Master Harold' . . . and the Boys, Blood Knot* (new version), *Hello and Goodbye, Boesman and Lena*; originally published as *Selected Plays* (Oxford: Oxford University Press, 1987), with same pagination

RM   *The Road to Mecca* (London, Boston: Faber & Faber, 1985)

SR   *Sorrows and Rejoicings* (New York: Theatre Communications Group, 2002)

TP   *The Township Plays*, ed. and intro. Dennis Walder (1993; repr. with a preface by Athol Fugard, Oxford: Oxford University Press, 2000); comprises *No-Good Friday, Nongogo, The Coat, Sizwe Bansi Is Dead, The Island*

VS   *Valley Song* (London: Faber & Faber, 1996)

Note on Terminology

Apartheid in South Africa encouraged an essentializing of racial or ethnic difference that resulted in both confusion and offence. Thus 'Native' was used for Bantu-speaking (Xhosa, Zulu, etc.) people of African origin, and 'European' for people of European origin, no matter how distant. 'Black' is nowadays often used for Africans, Indians or Asians, and 'Coloureds' – the last of mixed ethnic origin, including African, Khoisan, white, Chinese and/or Malay. Many Coloured people (predominantly in the Cape) call themselves Coloureds, while others prefer Black (or black). I have tried to clarify my usage by context, resisting terms like 'so-called'.

Introduction

Athol Fugard is South Africa's most important and prolific playwright, and the first to enjoy an international reputation. Yet his long and celebrated career is part of a much larger achievement: he has helped create a kind of drama that has established South African theatre as an arena in which audiences around the world have seen the emergence of a unique cultural form, drawn from the multiple traditions of Africa and Europe. Works by playwrights and practitioners as varied as Zakes Mda, Gcina Mhlophe, Mbongeni Ngema and Barney Simon, as well as groups such as the Serpent Players, Workshop '71, Junction Avenue Theatre Company and the Handspring Puppet Company, have engaged with the immediate issues of the time through collaborative workshop techniques and a stirring mix of improvisation, mime, dance, music and document. Migrant labour, child abduction, school rebellion, police torture, illegal strikes, township removals, imprisonment without trial and, more recently, the drama of the Truth and Reconciliation Commission: these have all been grist to the theatrical mill in South Africa. If there is one common impulse, it has been the urge to tell a story; and not just to tell a story, but to bear witness. The idea of witness, with its overtones of truth and sacrifice, has particular power in the face of the darkest events of our times. It is an idea that suggests the potential of art to respond to such events, and to reach across the boundaries of class, race, gender and nation, without descending into facile universalism.

It is my aim here to consider how far and in what sense Fugard's work continues to act as witness. Certainly some of

1

the plays and performances of the apartheid years have not survived well – becoming at best historic in the sense that they once testified to the events of the day, thereby helping to create and sustain a culture of opposition when other forms of protest were muted or denied. Where Fugard's contribution continues to matter is in its persistent focus upon the marginalized, upon the ordinary people of his region, while developing a dramaturgy connecting the subjective, interior world of the individual with the public, impersonal space of politics, broadly considered.

In 1984, at the height of the crisis then facing the country, critic Njabulo Ndebele argued against the tendency for cultural production to focus exclusively, even voyeuristically, upon the spectacular violence of the apartheid regime; it was time, he urged, to 'rediscover the ordinary'.[1] By 1990, as the apartheid regime collapsed, political prisoners were released and it looked as if a 'new South Africa' was at last coming into being, ANC activist Albie Sachs provocatively proposed that 'our members should be banned from saying that culture is a weapon of struggle [. . . for] a period of, say, five years', a statement that, when published in a local newspaper, stimulated a noisy debate.[2]

The point is that, while acknowledging the role played by so-called protest literature in South Africa, the country's leading cultural critics have for some time now argued in favour of a broader definition of the significance and place of literary work, including drama. Fugard himself said in 1991 that, while South African theatre was unique because in no other country had there been 'as direct and electrifying a relationship' between 'the event on the stage and the social and political reality out in the streets', he himself was 'a storyteller, not a political pamphleteer'. It was, he said, frustrating to be labelled a 'political' artist, since that created an expectation that got in the way of people 'receiving the play I have written. Even more seriously [. . .] it takes away certain freedoms from me as a writer.' This was despite the fact that 'I can't find any area of my living which politics has not invaded' (P. 71–3). While conservative critics sometimes see his plays as autonomous works of art, even they cannot ignore the varying ways in which they have been received, nor the impact they have had.[3]

2

There can be no doubt, for example, that Fugard's collab-orative work with performers across racial divisions during the apartheid years helped legitimate black experience as a vital form of cultural expression, and in this respect his influence has remained powerful. Moreover, his work can still shake audiences into attending to the silencings and oppressions of the present as well as the past, the present of 'truth and reconciliation' that recalls the private pains as well as the public gains of recent years.

I will be discussing his plays in terms of these different aspects: starting with his exploration of close family situations or relationships so as to draw in the wider tensions of his place and society; going on to examine the collaborative, and often directly political, 'township witnessing', as I call it; which coincided with a less well-known or appreciated quest on his part for more intimately profound, even mythic, 'carnal realities'; followed by, finally, the more recent, subjective, 'memory' plays. Labels tend to be reductive, but I hope this may be a way of capturing the 'very precarious balancing act' Fugard says he has been performing on the 'tightrope' of his 'writing life': between the 'two safe platforms' of the 'private and the public, the personal and the political'.[4]

As the image of himself on a tightrope suggests, Fugard's commitment to the theatre is total, and involves a willingness to take risks: not only on the personal level, but as a working playwright, director and actor at times when the rulers of his country seemed hell-bent on destroying, not only serious opposition, but all signs of independent thought. Family, friends and theatrical collaborators faced censorship, surveil-lance and worse, although, as Fugard acknowledges, he himself was protected from the most terrible aspects by the privilege of his white skin. It was the black members of his acting group who were imprisoned when there was a round-up in the Eastern Cape during the 1960s, not the playwright. The hegemony of the white minority created by apartheid meant that 'white liberals' and other dissidents were part of the structures of domination they opposed, although a distinction should always be made between their various forms of protest, compromised as it often was, and the willing submission to the system of most whites, and many blacks, over the years.

There are other complexities. Fugard has always been an advocate of 'poor theatre' on practical as much as on theoretical or political grounds. But he has been swept up within the mainstream he has long disregarded, or at least viewed with deep suspicion. At the beginning of the twenty-first century, his canonical status seems assured: most of his plays are in print – including the three volumes I have edited to scholarly standards – and several have been filmed or televised; he is widely performed and anthologized; his work is taught on school and university syllabuses in South Africa and abroad; and his manuscripts, notebooks and correspondence are lodged in a prestigious American university library (the Lilly Library, Indiana University). It was not always so. On 24 February 1963 the most influential theatre critic in Britain at the time, Kenneth Tynan, remarked in the *Observer* that Fugard's *The Blood Knot* merely reflected white guilt. It was a devastating verdict upon a playwright whose work had only just begun to make its way outside his own country, then increasingly viewed as an international pariah. But, as the playwright himself wryly remarked some thirty-four years later, at the South African premiere of his seventeenth full-length play, *The Captain's Tiger*: 'Today Tynan is in his grave and *The Blood Knot* isn't.'[5]

Fugard's drama not only raises the familiar issue of the troubled relationship between artists and their critics or reviewers; it also poses the problem of how to evaluate and respond to work that has, at different times, produced strikingly different, or opposed reactions – most notably, between the 'metropolitan', on the one hand, and the 'local', on the other. This is a crude distinction, often invoked by those 'postcolonial' critics who wish to argue the importance of local or national cultural products as against their devaluation by those who sit in judgement in distant centres of power, such as London or New York. Yet it is a distinction that highlights the importance of attending to the changing location and reception of his work, so as to understand how it has redefined the meaning of theatre in a situation of struggle, oppression – and, more recently, liberation. Ironically, since the early 1990s, Fugard has been more frequently produced abroad (especially in the USA) than in South Africa. Partly this is because other

4

playwrights have taken up writing about immediate local issues, such as the HIV / AIDS crisis and the drug culture of the townships (for example, Fatima Dike's *Streetwalking and Company* (2000)); partly it is because he has turned towards more persistently inward, autobiographical concerns (as in *The Captain's Tiger*); partly it is because he now spends much of his time with his family in the USA.

Fugard's work also reminds us of the importance of distinguishing between drama, as a written literary form, and theatre, as a staged performance – which, though usually including words, also involves space, props, actors, audience and the intricate relations between them at any particular moment. Recent literary theory has been more comfortable with drama than with theatre; post-colonial theory has barely bothered with either, with some exceptions. While a number of well-informed critics (such as Martin Banham, Michael Etherton and David Kerr) have written persuasively about African drama, relatively few have focused explicitly on the South African dimension. Of those who have, Temple Hauptfleisch deserves mention for his contribution to a developing history of *Theatre and Society in South Africa* (1997), and, on the more theoretical front, Martin Orkin (*Drama and the South African State* (1991)) and Loren Kruger (*The Drama of South Africa: Plays, Pageants and Publics since 1910* (1999)), who use the cultural materialism of Raymond Williams to question the politics of Fugard's theatrical impact, in particular how far his appeal to 'white liberals' may have compromised him. Brian Crow and Chris Banfield's *Introduction to Post-Colonial Theatre* (1996) places Fugard in the company of Derek Walcott and Wole Soyinka as 'major dramatists from the Third World', while arguing that his distinctive contribution has been to pioneer the multiracial 'workshop' play. This focus is shared with Helen Gilbert's and Joanne Tompkins's *Post-Colonial Drama: Theory, Practice, Politics* (1996), where a brief reference acknowledges the importance of performance, exemplified by *The Island*, the play Fugard created in private workshop conditions with two black actors about a two-man version of Sophocles' *Antigone* on Robben Island.[6]

The Island's production history clarifies the issues here. Depicting prison conditions at a time when such representations were forbidden, the work was not written down until it had been first performed (in 1973) before a small club audience in Cape Town in the presence of the police; and it required successful performance abroad, in London's Royal Court Theatre, for the kind of recognition that helped protect it from censorship at home. More recently, the play has reappeared, with its original actors and co-creators, John Kani and Winston Ntshona, before enthusiastic new audiences in Johannesburg (1995), Paris (1999), London (2000) and Toronto (2001). The Johannesburg production, before President Mandela and 300 former political prisoners, most of whom had never entered a theatre, concluded with both audience and cast singing the national (ANC) anthem. The (sell-out) London performances prompted the *Sunday Times* critic, John Peter, to exclaim:

> Who says that such plays are dated? Apartheid is gone but history is alive, the past lives in the present. This play belongs with Primo Levi's *If This is a Man*, Solzhenitsyn's *The First Circle*, Louis Malle's *Au Revoir les Enfants* and Dorfman's *Death and the Maiden*: great works of art that also bear witness to the darkest nights of the century with the precision of a documentary.[7]

After a time in which the world saw the suffering and annihilation of millions, it is often difficult to argue the claims of culture, especially something apparently as ephemeral as theatre. But if, as Baz Kershaw suggests (in *The Radical in Performance: Between Brecht and Baudrillard* (1999)), theatre in the West has lost its radical edge as a result of the collapse of traditional left-wing ideas of political theatre, on the one hand, and the promiscuity of the political in postmodern culture, on the other, then this kind of theatre suggests a model for the future.

I believe this to be so despite the fact that the applause for a play like *The Island*, even from new audiences, may prompt such questions as: are we responding to past defiance or present relevance? How far does the play really still 'bear witness'? Fugard himself has used this phrase since at least as early as 1968, when he was most absorbed in the left-liberal, European tradition of Albert Camus – a tradition kept alive by writers such as Anna Akhmatova and Primo Levi, but that, in

6

the specific South African context, should not simply be accepted prima facie. Bearing witness on behalf of others, however vital, may mean replacing their voices, speaking for them, rather than allowing them to speak. As has been pointed out, it is impossible to act as a transparent medium for the oppressed. Fugard's best work implicitly claims to speak on behalf of black people, and of women, but with how much justification? Does he pretend to be transparent? Fugard himself in these days of black empowerment claims to speak only for himself – and perhaps for 'the Afrikaner'.[8]

Yet at least one can say that reasserting the European tradition of witnessing in the South African context has one really important advantage for a dramatist, and that is the fact that the idea of witness carries with it an implication of present embodiment, derived from the Christian notion that testimony is provided by the physical presence, the suffering, even martyrdom (the Greek word for witness is *martus*), of the person, the *body* offering it. This relates immediately to Fugard's conception of performance, a conception according to which the ideal actor is a 'holy' figure, who will 'burn himself alive and wave to the audience through the flames'.[9] Behind such imagery lie notions of spiritual self-discipline and physical excess initiated by theatre-workers such as Antonin Artaud, Jerzy Grotowski and Peter Brook – themselves inspired by the theatre of non-Western cultures. Fugard's own emphasis upon disciplined physicality is also derived from the performance traditions he discovered among the untrained but enormously talented 'township' actors whose creative contribution to his career was crucial from the start. In this sense, his work provides the best demonstration of the syncretism urged by the first important black South African dramatist, Herbert Dhlomo (1903–56), who wrote that African drama 'must borrow from, be inspired by, shoot from European dramatic art forms'.[10]

This suggests the value of Fugard's kind of witnessing. As he once confided to his friend Mary Benson (1919–2000), his 'job' as a playwright was 'to witness as truthfully as I can, the nameless and destitute of one little corner of the world'.[11] Truth telling and witnessing are difficult and complex matters; but, as a general statement, subject to reinterpretation in the changing present, this represents a consistent position – even when, during the 1990s, it came to include reminiscing about his own personal past, in prose memoir as well as theatrical metaphor. There has always been an urge towards intimate revelation in his work, coinciding with a willingness to acknowledge the experiences of those excluded from wealth and power. Yet, in the end, what matters most to him are the moral imperatives of life in the face of death, rather than any specifically socio-political concern.

For Fugard, play writing is much more than just writing: it is an art form of the highest urgency for the individual, expressed in the concrete situation of theatrical performance, that 'of the actor and the stage, the actor *on* the stage. Around him is space, to be filled and defined by movement and gesture; around him is also silence to be filled with meaning, using words and sounds, and at moments when all else fails him, including the words, the silence itself.'[12] In his earlier days, that silence was the product of a multifarious and often frightening set of forces; but if, instead of heading towards the abyss, South Africa seems to have emerged 'through a gap into the sunlight', regaining 'the respect, even at times the affection, of a world that until recently was disposed to be hostile', the realities of the present 'are not quite as rosy as this', for, as the new millennium begins, it remains a violent, divided country, 'and the passage from that wonder year of 1990 has been far from easy'.[13] The process of change has been tougher than many anticipated, and yet the transformation of the country from a white-ruled, totalitarian state into a multiracial democracy proceeds apace, and the potential of theatre to expose repression, as well as celebrate survival, remains. This much has been lastingly demonstrated by Fugard's theatre.

1

Protest and Survival

Fugard's plays typically engage our sympathies for the fate of two or three marginalized characters closely entangled by the ties of blood, love or friendship, struggling to survive in a bleak and almost meaningless universe. This scenario is in part explicable in terms of his career and influences. His dark vision of pain never finally excludes the potential for humour and compassion, a potential expressed in the revelatory 'living moments' (N. 89) he always seeks from a production, as a means of 'bearing witness' – not only to what has happened to others, but to his own family experiences. If, as he once remarked, 'almost invariably' the provocation of a story has come 'from incidents and experiences outside of my personal life', he has needed 'a coincidence between the external story and a certain need in myself to articulate something about myself for the play to have been written'.[1] More recently, he has asserted that 'Not one of my plays has been driven by an "idea", political or otherwise. All of them have had their genesis in an image or incident, mostly from my own life but occasionally from second-hand sources' (Preface, *IP*). Some account needs to be given of these sources in the context of his career.

Harold Athol Lanigan Fugard was born on 11 June 1932, on a farm near Middelburg, Cape Province – a village in the semi-desert Karoo region of South Africa. His parents ran a small general dealer's store in Middelburg. His father, Harold, a former jazz pianist crippled in a work-related incident, was descended from English immigrants, possibly Irish-Huguenot in origin. His mother, Elizabeth Magdalena, née Potgieter, was a descendant of one of the foremost Voortrekker families, long settled in the Karoo. Fugard's parents came from different worlds within white settler culture. They were never well-off, and his mother supported the family. Like Albert Camus (1913–60), whom in some respects he resembles as well as admires, Fugard came from the underprivileged, barely literate sector of the white group, whose intolerance he rejects, while understanding its sources. Camus went into exile; Fugard stayed on, even when the regime tried to push him into taking a one-way 'exit permit' by rescinding his passport. He has always asserted that only while living where he was could he represent the reality of the lives of those around him.

Fugard has spoken of himself as of 'mixed descent' in white South African terms, 'culturally a bastard',[2] inheriting both the narrowly Calvinist but independent attitudes of his mother's background, and the more liberal attitudes of the English-speaking community, if not of his father. His mother's influence was the stronger, but, like many Cape Afrikaners, Fugard was educated in English; and, most significantly, he chose to write in English. Many of the characters in his plays would naturally speak Afrikaans (for example, Boesman and Lena in the play of that name); and their 'textures' are derived in the main from the Eastern Cape. At times, Fugard 'translates' their dialogue into English – or, more accurately, into a specifically Eastern Cape variety of South African English, drawn from Afrikaans and, sometimes, Xhosa speech, in a way that enables his work to be understood by a world audience, without sacrificing its local feel. But he has never thought of himself as an Afrikaans writer, in the sense that, say, the Eastern Cape playwright Reza De Wet has done.

In 1935 the family (including an older brother, Royal, and a younger sister, Glenda) moved to Port Elizabeth, an industrial port on the Eastern Cape seaboard, where they lived to begin with in a boarding house run by Mrs Fugard. Fugard recalls listening to his father play the piano in the Jubilee Residential Hotel, when 'I first savoured what were to become the two great addictions of my life – words and music' (C. 16). But it was the regular Sunday visits to his cousin Johnnie's house on the outskirts of the city that provided 'the first formative experiences that led to my career as a dramatist'. Johnnie would play the piano, while Hally (as he was called) listened, and waited for an image: 'It always came, and when it did I would turn it into words.' The two adolescent boys' 'musical stories' became performances for an obliging audience of admiring mothers. The importance of an initial, defining image, around which a narrative was woven to evoke a pattern of emotions, was thus established. 'The parallels between music and theatre as a whole, and not just my particular dramas, are very striking. Both have time, actual experienced time, as one of the major dimensions [. . .]' (C. 35–7).

Port Elizabeth was Fugard's home for most of his life, although a house in the Karoo village of Nieu Bethesda, thirty miles from Middelburg, has since the 1970s become a refuge, and in 2000 he finally sold his Port Elizabeth house. Short spells in larger centres such as Cape Town, Johannesburg, London, New Haven, New York and San Diego did not until the late 1990s draw him away from the Eastern Cape environment. In 1938 he entered the Catholic Marist Brothers College in Port Elizabeth. In 1941 his mother sold her rights in the Jubilee Hotel and invested in the centrally situated St George's Park Tearoom – the setting for 'Master Harold' . . . and the Boys (1982). Then, while his mother continued as the family's sole support, Hally began his secondary education on a council scholarship at the local Technical College, where he had his first experience of amateur dramatics, as actor and director of the school play – although he had also once helped supplement the family income with an 'apache dance' before overseas troops with his sister Glenda. A course in motor mechanics reflected an interest in motor cars, an interest emerging in his early novel Tsotsi (published 1980), a fantasy sequence in The Blood Knot (1961), a TV play Mille Miglia (1968) and Elsa's account of her long drive in the opening of The Road to Mecca (1984).

A scholarship took Fugard to the University of Cape Town, then one of the 'liberal', English-language universities of South Africa, where he was profoundly impressed by a Catholic existentialist Professor of Ethics, Martin Versfeld, another Cape Afrikaner. Central to Versfeld's thought was the problem of how it might be possible to communicate with, indeed love, one another, without exploitation. It is a question that often surfaces in Fugard's writings, as part of his struggle to connect

11

social awareness and individual responsibility. Fugard became a 'virulent little atheist' at university (C. 79), when his interest in Camus and existentialism began, as did his interest in evolution (explicit in *Statements after an Arrest under the Immorality Act* (1972), a play suggesting interracial love as part of an inevitable process). The Drama School at Cape Town is large and influential; Fugard's only involvement was a small role in a student production of Auden's and Isherwood's *The Ascent of F6* (1936). If his subjects of study (especially philosophy) were important to him, gaining a degree was not – or so he decided when, in June 1953, with a fellow advocate of existentialism, Perseus Adams, he set off north without a degree, but with £30 and ten tins of sardines. Upon reaching the Sudan, Fugard signed on as a 'captain's tiger' on the British tramp steamer *SS Graigaur* (an experience recalled in *The Captain's Tiger* (1997)).

Within a year (and an aborted attempt at a novel) he was back home, working as a freelance journalist for the Port Elizabeth *Evening Post*, which published (18 June 1954) his account of the struggles for education and self-fulfilment of black men and women from New Brighton township on the outskirts of the city. Fugard's concern to acknowledge the lives, indeed the very existence, of those of his compatriots excluded from the centres of power, and mired in poverty and oppression, thus manifested itself at the start of his career as a writer; but he had yet to find the right medium.

Fugard has remarked that the ten-month experience of living and working side by side with men of all races on the *Graigaur* liberated him from the prejudice endemic among those with his background. Nadine Gordimer once claimed that every white South African needs to be born twice: the second time into an awareness of racism.[3] For Fugard, unlike other white South African liberal writers, such as Gordimer, this meant effectively betraying his own people, which helps explain the painful, guilt-ridden fervour with which the racial issue is sometimes treated in his plays; and the reiterated assertion of his Afrikanerdom. He has traced his sense of guilt and remorse to an incident in his Port Elizabeth childhood, when he spat in the face of a black man – Sam Semela, who worked for the family over fifteeen years, and who was his 'most significant' friend. Yet such feelings helped to generate his plays, and that incident finally found a place forty years later in 'Master Harold' ... and the Boys, perhaps his most cathartic, confessional work (N. 25–6).

Fugard was first inspired to become actively involved in drama when he met his wife, Sheila Meiring, at the time a graduate of the University's Drama School, and an ambitious actress in Cape Town. Like Fugard, Sheila Meiring was half-Afrikaner, half-English; she later became a prominent South African novelist and poet. Fugard had obtained a post writing news bulletins for the South African Broadcasting Corporation in Cape Town, and was composing poetry and short stories in his spare time; but after his marriage to Sheila in September 1956 the theatre became his goal. A last-minute walk-on part in a production in which Sheila was playing (and Cape actor Yvonne Bryceland took the lead) was followed by the role of the messenger in an acclaimed version of Oedipus Rex. Thereafter the two formed an amateur theatre workshop, performing for a pittance on Sunday nights. Sheila directed and did most of the writing; her husband acted, then began to contribute short pieces, including The Cell, about a black woman who goes insane after giving birth in prison. No interest was expressed in the play, although, according to Sheila, 'Its lines had a beauty and its action an architecture that proclaimed a new writer.'[4] The writers to whom Fugard was drawn at this time, such as J. M. Synge, William Faulkner and Tennessee Williams, confirmed a growing sense that what he wanted to create was, above all, local.

But it was not until 1958, when the Fugards moved to Johannesburg, that this instinct began to find its true inspiration. The Fugards were introduced to the multiracial, inner-city township of Sophiatown by Benjamin Pogrund, a former student friend from Cape Town, and a journalist on the liberal Rand Daily Mail – whose new editor, Laurence Gandar, was about to galvanize anti-apartheid thinking with his forthright attacks on prison conditions. The only job Fugard could find at first was as clerk in a 'Native Commissioner's Court' where pass-law offenders were tried. It was a turning point. He knew his 'society was evil before', but 'seeing the machinery in operation taught me how it works and in fact what it does to

13

people'. Few white South Africans ever saw or became aware of what happened in such places. 'I think my basic pessimism was born there, watching that procession of faces and being unable to relate to them.'[5] Fugard's sense of alienation goes deep; and leads ultimately to an ethical and metaphysical, rather than political imperative. Nonetheless he was making his first black friends in the township, and out of their lives he created his first full-length, published plays: *No-Good Friday* (1958) and *Nongogo* (1959), both written for and performed by black amateurs.

There was only one white role, and that a small one, in these apprenticeship plays, which opened a window into urban black life for their (predominantly white) audiences. The key to life in the townships was (and is) survival; and this became a central theme. The Fugards created an African Theatre Workshop in Sophiatown, using Method techniques and drawing on the talents of a remarkable group of people, including the writers and journalists Lewis Nkosi, Bloke Modisane, Can Themba and Nat Nakasa, and one splendid actor – Zakes Mokae, a member of Father Trevor Huddleston's jazz group, and the first of Fugard's crucially important actor collaborators. 'Even then Athol was able to get astonishing performances out of these untried actors, who were on a stage for the first time in their lives.'[6] It was for Mokae that Fugard wrote the part of Zach in *The Blood Knot*, and it was upon his performance with Fugard that the play's immediate success depended. The idea for *The Blood Knot* came to Fugard in London in 1960, the year of the Sharpeville massacre – a turning point in relations between the apartheid state and the world. Thereafter, as the government cracked down on dissent, resistance seemed useless, except by indirect or violent means.

This is the context for Fugard's work over the succeeding three decades, work that, as he put it in a 1971 interview, was aimed at 'defiance: yes, my object is to defy. I am protesting against the conspiracy of silence about how the next man lives and what happens to groups other than our own [. . .] Yet I have never belonged to a political party or been a member of a banned organization.'[7] The small success of the Sophiatown plays had enabled Fugard – with the help of a visiting Belgian director, Tone Brulin – to obtain his first work in the professional theatre, as stage manager with the then all-white National Theatre Organization of South Africa. In a few months, he worked on plays by Shaw, Beckett, Ionesco, Pirandello and the South African James Ambrose Brown. The Sophiatown group had collapsed with the mass removals from the township and the departure of its members, many of whom went abroad. The Fugards also left for Europe, but returned after Fugard was turned down by the Royal Court Theatre in London (and acted in a play about 'trying for white' at an Avant-garde Theatre Festival in Brussels). Going back was an act of solidarity with his troubled country, but also ensured *The Blood Knot* would have the local textures Fugard needed.

This was more than a matter of Method. In the – mainly American – development of the Method approach, the tendency was to rely on naturalistic performances of pre-existing texts, constructed according to the familiar hierarchy of writer, director and actor. In Fugard's work, this was how *No-Good Friday* and *Nongogo* were conceived. But, although naturalism remains important, he usually heightens it, often moving away towards a more characteristically modern, symbolic realm, as in the work of Samuel Beckett – a major influence. After he and Zakes Mokae had performed the first version of *The Blood Knot* in a Johannesburg factory warehouse, they toured the country, travelling separately so as not to break apartheid laws, then acting together, before entranced audiences – both multiracial and white – in mainly unofficial venues, including the townships. A key local influence was Barney Simon (1932–95), Fugard's 'third eye' (assistant director) on *The Blood Knot*, and the influential director of many of his later plays. He had met the Fugards in 1959, just before they left for Europe, having himself already visited London, where he worked with Joan Littlewood and developed a passion for her small-scale, workshop projects. Simon was the only talent in white South African theatre to provide Fugard with any significant stimulus. He has never mentioned the mini-'renaissance' of English South African drama of the 1950s, including plays by Alan Paton, Lewis Sowden and Basil Warner – the last of whom wrote a play, *Try for White* (1959), which anticipated the subject of *The Blood Knot*.

15

Barney Simon shared Fugard's obsession with the textures of everday life, and, as a director, his willingness to transgress apartheid boundaries to discover and display the people's stories – hence Simon's later involvement in the founding of the Market Theatre (with Mannie Manim), in 1976, a space committed to avant-garde and independent work before multi-racial audiences. Where Fugard departed from Simon's emphasis upon the local and the everyday was in his interest in the mythical – or, at least, the early myths of the classical Greek era, the bloody family feuds dramatized by Aeschylus, Sophocles and Euripides, and reworked by many later dramatists, including Camus. Hence the little-known work entitled *Orestes*; hence the use of *Antigone* in *The Island*. But, unlike Camus (who, however, worked initially with two Algerian companies), Fugard was also open to a nearer tradition: the storytelling of black performers. White entrepreneurs in 1950s Johannesburg were aware of, and exploited, urban black popular performance traditions of storytelling, song and dance, of satire and jazz, which became more generally familiar with the emergence in 1959 of the jazz opera *King Kong*. But it was not until the 1970s and 1980s that there emerged a flood of 'township drama', from Gibson Kente's *Too Late* (1975) and Ngema / Mtwa / Simon's *Woza Albert!* (1981) to Gcina Mhlophe's *Have You Seen Zandile?* (1986), as the effects of censorship, bannings, imprisonment and exile were over-taken by many voices speaking out, simultaneously affirming their identity and the value of their culture.

Fugard was one of the first to recognize and respond to the creativity pent up for so long within the pressures of the apartheid system. Although blacks used to visit theatres before the National Party's victory in 1948, they sat in separate areas; by the early 1960s they were prohibited by law from attending performances, and 'mixed' casts were forbidden. Fugard's collaborative theatre practice challenged all this; hence it is no surprise that his influence upon black theatre specifically, as well as South African theatre more broadly, has been so strong. Playwrights living in the townships have learned tough lessons in survival, lessons articulated in many forms, using whatever means they can – including relationships with those such as Fugard, Simon and others willing and able to move

16

beyond their positions of privilege to provide artistic and economic support. Some township playwrights, such as Kente, always went their own way, creating musical melodramas for township audiences that were as popular as they were conventional; others, such as Matsemela Manaka and Maishe Maponya, drew on Brecht to inflect indigenous traditions with overt messages about living conditions for black people.

Fugard's instinctual recognition of the importance of the lives, the very being, of the 'other' preceded his debt to those amateurs first befriended in Sophiatown. But the experiences he tried to embody in *No-Good Friday* and *Nongogo* anticipated a second, much longer and more fruitful phase of collaborative work, which began with the arrival at his door one day in 1963 of a group of enthusiasts from the New Brighton township, 'with the old, old request', as the playwright confided to his notebooks at the time: 'actually it is hunger. A desperate hunger for meaningful activity – to do something that would make the hell of their daily existence meaningful' (*N.* 81). Fugard's acceptance of the challenge led to the Serpent Players, whose work with him produced (amongst other plays, including a version of Camus's *The Just*) *The Coat, Sizwe Bansi Is Dead* and *The Island.*

These works arose when the Players' practice was confronted by Fugard's reading of Grotowski (whose New York lectures were sent him by Benson in 1970). The result was his most 'extreme excursion' into radical communication by means of image and gesture, rather than pre-established text: *Orestes*, the separate performances of which are 'scored' in three large drawing books, a pale shadow of the eighty minutes of strange, somnambulistic action that took place at the time (1971). Here Fugard attempted an apparently total reliance upon the 'creative' as opposed to merely 'illustrative' abilities of his cast, two women and a man. Yet the 'truth' discovered was the result of the performers responding to the director-scribe's challenges, expressed as a complex of images Fugard derived from ancient and modern sources. This new type of theatre focused on an event close to white liberal protestors at the time: the explosion of a bomb on Johannesburg station in 1964, which killed a child and burnt an elderly white woman, and led to the execution of its perpetrator, a white schoolteacher.

17

Orestes represents an extreme, even a limit, to what Fugard has been able to create in the theatre. The play explored the effect of violence upon those who carry it out: the central image was created by the slow, deliberate and silent destruction in each performance of a unique, irreplaceable and innocent object – a chair – by the actor (Yvonne Bryceland), who sank down eventually into the debris, exhausted and terrified by what she had done. It was the same message as Camus's *The Just*: when, if ever, is violence justified? Fugard has always condemned violence, while implying its inevitability in a society that adopted violent means to stifle opposition and prevent change. Many whites admitted the contradictions and injustices of the apartheid system, including 'liberals' like Fugard. Liberalism is an attitude rather than a party, although he once admitted that if 'the old Liberal Party of South Africa still existed, I'd feel obliged to identify with it'.[8] The 'old Liberal Party' disbanded in 1968, when multiracial political parties became illegal. The liberal viewpoint emphasizes the value and dignity of the individual, an attitude reflected in a tradition of deep human concern, and resistance towards authoritarianism. These values survive, although South African liberals have often been accused (especially by those further on the left) of a naive faith in the reforming potential of personal moral pressure, and a failure to recognize the dynamics of power. Some white liberals were sympathetic towards extraparliamentary strategies such as passive resistance, boycotts and strikes – adopted perforce by the black opposition movements.[9]

Fugard lasted through all this, often under pressure (including threats, interrogation and surveillance), while holding onto a despairing hope for tolerance and decency. In 1962, an open letter to British playwrights led to an international playwrights' boycott of performances of their work in South Africa's segregated theatres. Fugard's passport was taken away in 1967, 'for reasons of state safety and security', after a performance of *The Blood Knot* on British television. He continued to write, direct and perform, until 1971, when a public petition of 4,000 signatures obliged the government to permit him to direct *Boesman and Lena* in Britain; thereafter his passport was returned. Meanwhile, in 1968, he sparked controversy by arguing (in vain) that the situation would be better served by abandoning the boycott, since, as he wrote to Mary Benson (who was appalled by this turnaround), 'all significant opposition has been silenced' and so: 'Anything that will get people to think and feel for themselves, that will stop them delegating these functions to the politicians, is important to our survival. Theatre can help do this' (N. 159). Some prominent theatre people (such as Janet Suzman) still argue that the boycott was a mistake, fatally narrowing South African cultural life even more than government restrictions. In my view, the boycott movement promoted that wider awareness of the effects of apartheid that helped to bring the system down in the end. In any case, Fugard came to believe that it was better to continue producing his work even in venues where all races could not attend – a decision he admits involved compromise.[10]

His overriding concern is with how people get trapped by the roles society creates for them – most sharply and oppressively, but not uniquely, in racial terms in a racist environment. In *The Blood Knot*, the two 'mixed-race' brothers finally appear reconciled to the roles allotted them by how they are perceived, although not without struggle. In *People Are Living There*, the central character, Milly, became the first of a series of attempts to invest in a woman the possibility of affirmation. Dealing with a group of (unusually) four characters in a Johannesburg boarding house, *People* led to the playwright's discovery of Yvonne Bryceland, cast as Milly on the advice of Barney Simon for what became a much-acclaimed production, mounted by the Cape Performing Arts Board in June 1969. For Fugard, 'poor-white' characters like Milly are objects of understanding, rather than condemnation, as he showed in *Hello and Goodbye* (1968), in which the possibility of defiance, if not escape, is hinted at, in the harsh vitality of Hester, especially as performed by Yvonne Bryceland, in a landmark production directed by the author for The Space in 1974, with Bill Flynn as Johnnie. Until her untimely death in 1992, Bryceland went on to play all Fugard's best roles for women – some of which she herself helped devise, like that of Frieda, the unmarried librarian whose interracial affair is at the centre of *Statements after an Arrest under the Immorality Act*, Clytemnestra in *Orestes*, and Sophia, the stoic housekeeper of *Dimetos* (1975).

19

In 1971, after securing his passport, Fugard accepted an invitation from South African Nicholas Wright to direct *Boesman and Lena* at the Royal Court Theatre Upstairs in London, with Bryceland as Lena, Mokae as Boesman and writer Bloke Modisane as Outa. The production was an immediate success, and the interest of Ross Devenish, an expatriate South African freelance film-maker, was aroused. He persuaded Fugard to collaborate on a film version, with Fugard himself and Bryceland in the title roles. The success of *Boesman and Lena* at the Edinburgh and London Film Festivals in the autumn of 1973 led to further work together, and the televising of other Fugard plays in South Africa. Devenish directed *The Guest at Steenkampskraal*, Fugard's account of an episode in the life of the tormented Afrikaans poet and amateur zoologist Eugène Marais (1871–1936), premiered on BBC2 TV on 5 March 1977, with Fugard in the main role; and in 1979 Devenish and Fugard made the film *Marigolds in August* on location near Port Elizabeth, with John Kani and Winston Ntshona. Film-making is not remotely as meaningful as theatre for Fugard, and the later, unimpressive adaptation of *The Road to Mecca*, with Fugard, Bryceland and Kathy Bates in the central roles, has proved the point.

The response of the Royal Court – in particular that of its moving spirit, Oscar Lewenstein – was then of great importance to Fugard. The freedom and commitment that characterized the English Stage Company had made the Court a desirable place in which to work from the time of Fugard's earlier London visit. By the mid 1970s, as a result of Lewenstein's faith in his potential, the Court was offering the public a 'South African Season', including the three 'Statements' plays, *Sizwe Bansi Is Dead*, *The Island*, and *Statements after an Arrest*, which became the foundation of Fugard's reputation abroad, as well as that of his co-creators and actors on these plays, Yvonne Bryceland, John Kani and Winston Ntshona. Fugard's courage and conviction as a total man of theatre was never sufficient on its own. By definition, since theatre is a collaborative art, it requires others – performers, as well as a place in which to perform. The Royal Court offered a special area of trust, 'a space that allowed me to make mistakes'.[11] It was something he had long yearned to have in South Africa.

Back home after the first overseas production of *Boesman and Lena* in 1971, he had begun discussions with Bryceland's husband, Cape Town photographer Brian Astbury, on forming an experimental theatre and obtaining a site at which to perform new plays. In March 1972 a new chapter in the history of South African theatre began with the opening in a converted warehouse near the old Malay quarter of Cape Town of the Space / die Ruimte / Indawo – its English name derived from the Open Space in Tottenham Court Road, London, as well as from Peter Brook's *The Empty Space* (1968). With the Market in Johannesburg, the Space became the venue for all that was exciting in South African theatre outside the black townships for the next seven years.

Sometimes the Space played host to the best of 'township drama', such as *Imfuduso*, created by the women of Crossroads, the infamous squatter camp on the outskirts of Cape Town; and it nurtured playwrights as varied as Fatima Dike, Geraldine Aron and Pieter-Dirk Uys; but it was Fugard's work that ensured initial success. An early version of *Statements after an Arrest*, with Fugard and Bryceland in the leading roles, was commissioned as the opening production; it was succeeded by *Sizwe Banzi [sic] Is Dead*, with a facsimile passbook as programme (the spelling of the title was altered after the first performance). The following year (1973) the first version of *The Island* (called *Die Hodoshe Span* to keep its location secret and avoid censorship) was conceived and rehearsed at the Space, while Fugard, Kani and Ntshona awaited passports for the *Sizwe Bansi* tour of Britain. Like the Market, the Space successfully evaded theatre segregation laws as well as censorship.

Fugard's career is marked by attempts to create a suitable space for a specifically African theatre; first there was the African Theatre Workshop in Sophiatown in 1958–9; then the New Africa Group in Brussels in 1960; an ill-advised visit to Lusaka in 1964 to direct *The Caucasion Chalk Circle*, abandoned as a result of conflict with the Zambian authorities; the Ijinle Company at the Hampstead Theatre Club, with Zakes Mokae and others, supposed to become a base for African theatre in London, but which folded after a production of Wole Soyinka's *The Trials of Brother Jero* in 1966; then the Space in Cape Town, which staggered on for years, despite the departure of Astbury and Bryceland for London, and its removal to new premises, but which eventually finally closed; followed by the Market Theatre, created by Simon and Manim in an old fruit market not subject to segregation laws, and an essential venue for Fugard, whose *A Lesson from Aloes* was premiered there in 1978; where *'Master Harold'* ... *and the Boys* had its local premiere in 1983; and where *The Road to Mecca* (1984), *A Place with the Pigs* (1987), *My Children! My Africa!* (1988), *Playland* (1992) and *Valley Song* (1995) all had their local premieres.

What is missing from all these later ventures is any significant involvement with black people, apart from Fugard's chosen performer, John Kani, in *My Children! My Africa!* and *Playland*. The history of the Serpent Players shows why. Within two years of their initial approach to Fugard, they had worked on five productions under his enthusiastic direction, rehearsing wherever they could. But on the day when their adaptation of *The Caucasian Chalk Circle* was due to open, the leading actor, Norman Ntshinga, was arrested, followed by several others – all tried, and imprisoned on Robben Island. Yet out of these events grew the making of plays without an identifiable author, improvization and new experiments with the creative potential of the actors – especially, with the two most gifted, who joined the Serpent Players in 1965 (John Kani) and 1967 (Winston Ntshona). *The Coat* was performed before a white 'theatre appreciation' group in Port Elizabeth in 1966, and was followed by many similar experiments, the most important of which turned out to be *Sizwe Bansi Is Dead* and *The Island*. The acclaim abroad for these two works enabled Kani and Ntshona to become successful performers in their own right, but it took them away from the Serpent Players – which, with its members in prison or harassed by the police, languished.

After the success of *Sizwe Bansi* and *The Island* during the early 1970s, a note of exhaustion appeared in Fugard's work. While events in South Africa were building up to the 1976–7 uprising, the playwright was turning inwards, towards more personal, abstract concerns – evident in the unpopular *Dimetos*, commissioned for the Edinburgh Festival in 1975. After more than ten years in their small bungalow at Schoenmakerskop, a

22

village perched upon a headland some miles south of Port Elizabeth, the Fugards retreated to a new home they built for themselves near Sardinia Bay, 'The Ashram' – a name reflecting Sheila Fugard's conversion to Buddhism. Here Fugard awaited new 'appointments' for some seven years, during which, like the middle-aged Afrikaner Piet Bezuidenhout in *A Lesson from Aloes* (1978), he felt increasingly isolated and ineffectual, although determined to survive, since, as Piet says: 'There's nothing you can do to stop a drought, but bad laws and social injustice are man-made and can be unmade by men' (*IP* 242). The playwright's continuing uncertainty was apparent in the appearance in 1980 of such ventures as the American playlet *The Drummer*, the film *Marigolds in August*, and the publication, after a twenty-year delay, of his novel *Tsotsi*; as well as assorted appearances as a film actor (for example, as General Smuts in Richard Attenborough's *Gandhi* (1982)). But this apparent lack of direction evaporated with the arrival of *'Master Harold' . . . and the Boys*, premiered on 12 March 1982 at the Yale Repertory Theatre and directed by the playwright himself. A six-month fellowship at Yale in 1980, when he assisted Mary Benson in editing his notebooks for publication, led to a ten-year theatrical relationship, and try-outs in New Haven before Broadway, or simultaneously with the National Theatre in London and the Market in Johannesburg.

By the time of *The Road to Mecca*, premiered at Yale in 1984, it had become clear that a new phase of play making had arrived, with Fugard returning to the more conventional, 'private' form of production (which he had never completely abandoned), writing plays before directing his chosen performers in a given, known and no longer marginal theatre space. Like *Aloes*, *Mecca* was set in an earlier period, avoiding any direct engagement with contemporary events, which, with the Declaration of a State of Emergency in 1984, were reaching a crisis. He chose to continue the trend set by *Dimetos*, and *The Guest* (and to a lesser degree, *'Master Harold'*): of exploring the psychology of the isolated white consciousness, figured as an artist. *Mecca* takes place in the glass-encrusted living room of a controversial Nieu Bethesda sculptress, 'Miss Helen' Martins.

The play implicitly registered a growing feminist politics in South Africa. It was not the first of Fugard's works to place such strong emphasis upon female relationships (*Dimetos* did that), nor the last (it is evident in *Sorrows and Rejoicings* (2001)); but it is the only play in which the central relationship is between two women. The resolution of past trauma for the two women in the play, however, masked the question left at the end: what about the 'good old South African story' of the destitute black woman? Her presence (based on a real encounter) prompted Fugard initially to name the play 'My English Name is Patience'. Race and gender issues become more overtly entangled in *My Children! My Africa!*, which featured a middle-aged township headmaster, 'Mr M', played by John Kani, newly associating with Fugard after several years working at the Market Theatre. *My Children! My Africa!* signalled a return to contemporary subject matter after its immediate predecessor, *A Place with the Pigs*, a 'personal parable' ostensibly about freeing oneself from base urges. *My Children! My Africa!* was a direct response to an event five years before – the murder on township streets in the Eastern Cape of a schoolmaster by youths who believed him a police collaborator. Audiences in South Africa and abroad responded favourably, but the huge enthusiasm that had greeted, say, *'Master Harold'* was lacking; and critical reaction was muted. Partly this was because, although the play demonstrated once again Fugard's power and authority in response to a contemporary issue – how far can one oppose tyranny without some form of personal betrayal – its concluding emphasis, upon a white girl's spiritual yearnings, while her black counterpart leaves for military training abroad, seemed forced.

Nevertheless, offering weight to all three voices, including the young woman's attack on patriarchy, suggested that Fugard was prepared to offer debate. Fugard wishes to mediate if not incorporate the voices of the submerged, voiceless 'other' within his plays, either literally, by collaborating with his carefully chosen performers, or more obliquely, by registering an inner sense of what has not yet been heard. The results can be disturbing, as in his depiction of a young man carrying the guilt of an atrocity on the South African border – Gideon le Roux – whose accidental meeting with a black nightwatchman in a travelling amusement park in the Karoo on New Year's Eve 1989 is at the centre of the ironically titled

Playland. Less well received in the USA and Britain than in South Africa, the play reflected local hopes and fears: hopes that the moves towards the new dispensation would wipe out the guilt and distress of the past; fears that the violence for so long attendant upon racial division and tension would resurface. Reconciliation between the two men at the end of *Playland* was as difficult to accept as that urged by political leaders in the years immediately succeeding Nelson Mandela's release in 1990 – years marked by continuing unrest throughout the country.

Yet, as in *The Blood Knot* (with which it has parallels), *Playland* probes the alternating relationship of dependency and struggle between characters caught within their historic social, racial and gender roles. In *My Life*, premiered at the Grahamstown National Arts Festival three months after the elections in May 1994, Fugard placed five young women from varying racial and cultural backgrounds on stage to perform extracts from their personal diaries – a performance shaped so as to present new audiences (the work toured schools) with their adolescent pathos and naivety, while speaking on their behalf for the transformation of the country and its new, gender-aware constitution. *My Life* coincided with a growing desire to tell his own story – a desire channelled into the memoir *Cousins*, before he placed himself on stage as the self-styled Author in his next play, *Valley Song*, encountering the struggle to self-expression of a young Eastern Cape 'Coloured' woman. This play offered a powerful critique of Fugard's attempts to speak on behalf of the voiceless, while appearing to manipulate the voices of others to serve his own interest in individual freedom and desire.

This shift in what has become possible for Fugard to articulate in post-election South Africa has led to even more personal and (some have argued) damagingly nostalgic work, such as the autobiographical three-hander, *The Captain's Tiger*, a reflection upon his early months in the merchant marine, premiered in the once racially exclusive State Theatre in Pretoria in 1997, with Fugard once again performing himself as Author, and (as in *'Master Harold'*) with his wounded father a troubling, invisible presence. Acknowledging the profound influence of Fugard's mother upon his creative imagination, the play nonetheless recalls the importance throughout his career of black performers and friends – in this case, an illiterate ship's mechanic who wants him to 'speak . . . also for me' (CT 74). Emerging from the playwright's distant past so as to pay a debt to the sources of his creativity, *Tiger* may be seen as a coda to *'Master Harold' . . . and the Boys*.

The interweaving of past and present that has become the dominant note in Fugard's work may continue; but, in any case, the South African experience offered in his plays is where he begins and ends: bitter, and often painful to contemplate, but also radiating humour, it expresses a deep faith in the potential for survival of the individual human being. Many years ago he stated that 'bearing witness' meant simply that, as a South African,

> I want to talk to other South Africans about what is happening here and now. Now, being a South African means that I have got to acknowledge the fact that my whole style of living, everything, comes down to . . . how many decisions have I got that are not related to my white skin? I can only acknowledge that these exist, that they are facts . . . Thorn trees don't protest the endless drought of the Karoo. [. . .] They just go on trying to grow. Just a basic survival informs the final, mutilated, stunted protest.[12]

These are words that can well stand as his credo. His plays are not written as protest in the usual sense, a fact that has led to attack from the more politically committed, in South Africa and abroad. Nor are they 'universal', in the sense that they reflect the Western values and interests of critics who thus label them. Instead, they negotiate the troubled and troubling terrain between: from within the codes and textures of South Africa, they reach out to whoever is open to the exploration of what the theatre in the modern world can do to define our anxieties about ourselves and our relations to others.

2

Plays of Place

The idea of place has become increasingly important in discourses concerning colonial and post-colonial cultural activity. This phenomenon responds to the effacing of the local and particular by the colonizing imagination, an ethnocentric view of the world that underpinned control and exploitation from within, as well as from the old imperial centres of power. Unfortunately, in reacting against this monolithic, globalizing tendency, post-colonial criticism has tended to downplay the existential realities of people in the former colonized territories, with the result that the contingent particularities that create the potential of witnessing in Fugard's work are easily neglected. But the rootedness of his work in a specific locale is one key to his achievement; his urge to represent the marginalized is inseparable from their time, and place. In the plays discussed here, that impulse or compulsion is realized on two levels: by representing others, and by representing himself and his family.

Thus Fugard's first important play, *The Blood Knot* (1961, later revised as *Blood Knot*, 1985),[1] was also the first of five to be set 'where I grew up, where I have spent the major part of my life, and where my imagination has flourished': that is, in Port Elizabeth, in the Eastern Cape. The 'specifics' or 'codes' of that part of South Africa are what have defined him and his voice 'irrevocably' (Preface, *PEP*). Port Elizabeth, founded by the 1820 British settlers, is a fairly representative South African place, containing nearly a million people, about one-third of whom are mainly English-speaking whites, two-thirds of whom used to be classified 'non-white' – mainly Xhosa-speaking black people, but also Chinese, Indians and 'Coloureds' (people of mixed race: a term still widely used of themselves, without offence). These putative 'non-whites' were, under apartheid, legally obliged to live in 'locations' or 'townships' on the city fringes, near the major industries they served – the most important of which was the motor-car industry (Ford set up there in the 1920s); they also constituted a vast army of labourers and servants. Censorship reinforced a divided cultural life: for the theatre, this differentiation meant occasional visiting overseas and local productions for whites, while blacks made their own entertainments in church or community halls. A series of proclamations and laws against racially mixed audiences and performers culminated in the 1963 Publications and Entertainments Act (rescinded a quarter of a century later), which had the paradoxical effect of stimulating the growth of Black Consciousness Theatre from the late 1960s onwards, including plays like Mthuli Shezi's *Shanti* (1973).

For all that they were generated by and for black township audiences, however, such works were influenced by Fugard's interracial, 'township' plays, initiated by his experiences in Sophiatown, but then after 1963 by the New Brighton Serpent Players, whose practice will be analysed in the next chapter. What is most striking about the plays analysed here is that they are concerned with the borderline, 'Coloured' or 'poor-white' areas of the city: the product of Fugard's fixation not only with his place, but also with his family, as a site of powerlessness and ambivalence. First focusing on brother and brother (*The Blood Knot/Blood Knot*), then brother and sister (*Hello and Goodbye*) and then (in *Boesman and Lena* and *A Lesson from Aloes*) man and woman as partners/spouses. Although the much later *'Master Harold' . . . and the Boys* is set in central Port Elizabeth, its claim to kinship of the black and Coloured people of the four earlier works is expressed in terms of a confessional format, which links it more closely with the plays discussed later, in Chapter 5. The central male role in all these plays (Morris, Johnnie, Boesman, Piet and Hally) is derived to a greater or lesser extent from the author's acknowledged self-reflection, while the women (Hester, Lena and Gladys) more diffusely reflect sister and wife. The plays move towards a theatre of witness as memory and revelation.

The central issue, as *The Blood Knot/Blood Knot* suggests from the start, is what Hegel identified as the problem of recognition. For Hegel, all consciousness involves 'the desire to be recognized and proclaimed as such by other consciousnesses', which leads to a view of human relations as 'a perpetual struggle, to the death, for recognition of one human being by another'. This struggle, says Camus, projected onto the history of humanity, is 'in its essence, imperialist'; it is also 'absurd', since, in the event of one consciousness being destroyed by the will to power of another, the victorious consciousness 'cannot be victorious in the eyes of something that no longer exists'. Hence absurdity, rather than tragedy, is the end of human endeavour, which, in the Hegelian system, requires two kinds of consciousness at the outset: that of the 'master', who obtains recognition from the other, thereby becoming independent, and that of the 'slave', who provides that recognition, but at the cost of becoming an 'object'. 'They are distinguished one from the other at the moment when they clash and when one submits to the other.'[2]

Such a moment occurs at the climax of the first Port Elizabeth play, *The Blood Knot/Blood Knot*, when the two Coloured brothers, Zach (the 'darker') and Morris (the 'lighter'), whose behaviour is plotted in terms of a mutual desire for recognition, enact their final clash. The succeeding plays conform to this alternating thematic pattern, exploring the tensions generated by relations of power and dependency between two or three people. In *Hello and Goodbye*, the sister finally releases herself from the emotional trap in which her brother remains, clinging to the image of their dead father; in *Boesman and Lena*, the couple play out an exchange of dominant and submissive roles to an extreme of exhaustion and despair; in *A Lesson from Aloes*, husband and wife accept their unequal roles, at the cost of impotence and madness; while, in '*Master Harold*' . . . *and the Boys*, the white teenager of the title learns how the person who most effectively fulfils the role of father is one of the black men defined as his 'boy'.

This complex and shifting pattern is rooted in all the specific, often fiercely comic detail of the lives of the impoverished, discarded inhabitants of Port Elizabeth, whom Fugard knows so well; yet it also suggests an existential dimension to that urge to survive, if not transcend, their situation, which marks many of his characters. They do not rebel, in Camus's sense; but they do strive to go beyond resignation and despair in the secular world to which they are condemned – a striving suggested by the imagery of flying, as a bird (in *The Blood Knot/Blood Knot* and *Boesman and Lena*) or (in *'Master Harold'*) a kite. There are religious overtones to these and some of the later plays, such as *Road to Mecca*. But religion in Fugard's work offers no security; its overt manifestations are the product of guilty anguish or a desire to control.

The original play *The Blood Knot* was conceived at the time of the Sharpeville massacre, on the cusp of a new and bloody era; yet it began simply as a Port Elizabeth setting, drawn from memory, in these notes made in London:

> Korsten: The Berry's Corner bus, then up the road past the big motor-assembly and rubber factories. Turn right down a dirt road – badly potholed, full of stones, donkeys wandering loose, Chinese and Indian grocery shops – down this road until you come to the lake. Dumping ground for waste products from the factories. Terrible smell. On the far side, like a scab, Korsten location. A collection of shanties, pondoks, lean-to's. No streets, names, or numbers. A world where anything goes.[3]

That world becomes the site of the seven-scene play, finally written as a 'compulsive and direct experience' on Fugard's return to South Africa.[4] In its shabby indeterminateness, brutal anonymity and moral chaos, the 'location' (township) is a place beyond the control of the authority that creates it, yet that defines its people as less than human.

The play begins in a run-down but neat shack, which will be the place of the whole action. A shabby, light-skinned man carefully prepares a footbath, timing his actions, evidently routine, with an old alarm clock; an equally shabby dark-skinned man, wearing an old greatcoat, comes slouching in, looking exhausted. He makes a great show of being surprised by the footbath, testing it with one toe, and so on, before finally and luxuriously resting his calloused feet in it. In that silent but physically eloquent gesture, a relationship is established that has disturbing implications: it reveals what appears to be a white man behaving like a housekeeper, a servant, to a black. According to witnesses of the first, four-hour performance in

30

the so-called Rehearsal Room,[5] the effect was deeply shocking, challenging the power relationship central to the structure of South African society. Adding to the frisson for the invited, multiracial audience was the fact that Fugard, with his shaggy hair and spade-like black beard, his wiry figure encased in torn old clothes, looked the image of a bedraggled Voortrekker – an image confirmed by Morris's dream of creating a farm in 'one of those blank spaces' on the map of Africa (*PEP* 59–61), and by his literal-minded faith in the word of the Bible:

> [*Alarm-clock rings.*] Bed time. [*Takes down his Bible.*] My turn to choose the reading tonight, Zach. [*Chooses a passage.*] Matthew. I like Matthew. [*Reads.*] 'And Asa begat Josaphat, and Josaphat begat Joram, and Joram begat Ozias; and Ozias begat Joatham, and Joatham begat Achaz, and Achaz begat Ezekias; and Ezekias begat Manasses, and Manasses begat Amon, and Amon begat [. . .]' [*Pause.*] That must have been a family. (*PEP* 72)

Our laughter is tempered by a sense that this reveals the inherited settler Calvinism continuing in their mixed-race offspring – two brothers tied together by the blood of the title, begat within an environment in which differences of appearance determine what they can do, and may hope for.

The ideology of difference was upheld by an unholy alliance between the apartheid state and the Dutch Reformed Church, an ideology encouraging the lighter-skinned Morris to 'pass for white' while generating endless guilt for having done so. The characterization of Morris as literate and prudent, using his Bible and alarm clock to control his darker brother, Zachariah, who, by contrast, is physically at ease with himself, sensual and illiterate, has been criticized as racial stereotyping. But the play overturns such assumptions.

Zach earns their keep as a factory worker relegated to gate-watchman, while Morris tends house, saves for their future and attempts to impart the virtues of routine, conversation and brotherly love – virtues that keep his brother under his spell. But, when Zach begins to rebel, Morris conceives the plan of getting his brother to take up with 'a corresponding pen-pal of the opposite sex' (*PEP* 64). The plan backfires: Ethel Lange of Oudtshoorn, 'eighteen years old and well-developed', who wishes to correspond with 'a gent of sober habits and a

31

good outlook on life', is white (*PEP* 69–70) and wants to visit. Why not? Morris warns Zach: 'They don't like these games with their whiteness.'

> ZACHARIAH. What have I done, hey? I done nothing.
> MORRIS. What have you thought, Zach! That's the crime [. . .] And what about your dreams, Zach [. . .] When they get their hands on a dark-born boy playing with a white idea, you think they don't find out what he's been dreaming at night? They've got ways and means, Zach. Mean ways. Like confinement, in a cell, on bread and water, for days without end. They got time. All they need for evidence is a man's dreams [. . .]
>
> (*PEP* 92)

Many of Fugard's characters are dreamers, whose dreams are doomed – not only by the threat of detentions and interrogation, but also by the limits of racialized perception.

Zach thinks the way out of their dilemma is to persuade his brother to stand in for him, and play the white man, using their savings to buy an outfit 'for a gentleman' (*PEP* 100). Morris points out that 'There's more to wearing a white skin than just putting on a hat [. . .] this whiteness of theirs is not just in the skin, otherwise . . . well, I mean . . . I'd be one of them, wouldn't I?' (*PEP* 103). So much for stereotyping: the play reflects the malign absurdity of the shifting, yet historically and culturally bound signifier of race, everywhere apparent in the apartheid laws – in one year, for example, 795 people officially 'changed race', including 518 former Coloureds who became white, two whites who became Chinese, one white who became Indian, eighty-nine Africans who became Coloured, and five Coloureds who became African. Categories such as 'appearance' and 'acceptability', which were introduced to make things clearer, only increased the uncertainty; a white becoming a person who

> a. In appearance obviously is a white person and who is not generally accepted as a Coloured person; or
> b. Is generally accepted as a white person and is not in appearance obviously not a white person.[6]

The Blood Knot/Blood Knot suggests the degree to which, in societies with long histories of exploiting constructions of difference to maintain and extend inequalities of power, the sense of identity is not just a matter of 'negotiation' (as many literary-cultural theorists would have it), but a site of existential uncertainty and struggle – not to say of life and death.[7]

Inevitably, the original impact of Fugard's play depended to some extent upon the system of race discrimination then being enforced throughout South Africa. But neither the word apartheid, nor any specific reference to it, appears in this play. Instead, the underlying conflict moves to its conclusion, as the lighter-skinned brother Morris participates in their 'game' and acts the white boss, abusing his inferior. 'Where are you?' cries Morris.

> ZACHARIAH. Behind a tree
> MORRIS. But . . . but I thought you were the good sort of boy?
> ZACHARIAH. Me?
> MORRIS. Weren't you that? The simple, trustworthy type of John-boy? Weren't you that?
> ZACHARIAH. I've changed.
> MORRIS. Who gave you the right?
> ZACHARIAH. I took it!
>
> (PEP 121)

In earlier performances, the transformation of the obsequious 'John boy' into the aggressor seemed the familiar stalking horse of fearful white imaginations. However, as performed for example by black British actor Gordon Case – a big man with an aura of calm authority – in the 1999 London production, it became a confident assertion of the right for recognition.

If such sequences do not always shock or provoke as they once did, the potential of *The Blood Knot/Blood Knot* to survive in different times and places remains; a potential summed up by *The Times*'s Benedict Nightingale, who sarcastically observed (on 12 April 1999): 'The play is of course *dreadfully dated* at a time when, as events from Eltham to Kosovo to mid-Africa have been confirming, all our ethnic, tribal and fratricidal problems are happily resolved.' Nightingale's reference to Eltham was particularly telling to an audience keenly aware not only of Kosovo and Rwanda, but also of the south London suburb where black teenager Stephen Lawrence was murdered in 1993 by a group of white youths chanting racist slogans. The failure of the resulting police investigation led to a public inquiry, which revealed gross incompetence and racism in the Metropolitan Police force, as a result of which police activities in Britain were for the first time made subject to anti-racist laws.

By exploring the way in which difference is constructed, dramatizing the implications of that construction with realistic detail, humour and symbolic force, *The Blood Knot/Blood Knot* still connects itself with our changing times. Remarks such as Morris's 'this whiteness of theirs is not just in the skin ... otherwise ... well, I mean, I'd be one of them, wouldn't I?' (*PEP* 103), or the horrifying moment in the play when both men turn on and stone their mother (*PEP* 118), in Loren Kruger's words 'the unseen scapegoat'[8] of the play – such moments still call for a response, a witnessing, on a level beyond, while including, apartheid.

The play encourages audiences to acknowledge the construction of difference on a deep level, connecting with communities wherever people who look and sound alike to the outsider have among themselves created deadly barriers of difference. The relationship between two men of mixed-race parentage in a country where race is a marker of power and privilege becomes a debate about the nature of self and other in a world without universals; yet the play's survival value lies in its witness to the secret yearnings for recognition, and for the freedom to escape from the internalized boundaries created within and between people, in our various but historically specific situations.

I have dwelt on *The Blood Knot/Blood Knot* at some length because not only is it one of Fugard's earliest and greatest plays, but it established his kind of theatre: a small cast of marginal characters presented in a circling, repetitive but passionately close relationship embodying the tensions of their society, often first performed by actors directly involved in its creation, in a fringe or at least non-mainstream theatre. Much closer to Beckett than to Brecht, Fugard has learnt from both in sustaining a theatrical practice of subtle, multilayered plays that express a demand recognized by audiences, reviewers and critics – sometimes by avoidance, as when some earlier reviewers refused to acknowledge *The Blood Knot*'s connection with 'the race problem'.[9]

Fugard completed a first draft of his next play, *People Are Living There*, as the original *Blood Knot* tour of South Africa came to an end in 1963; but it was not until 1968 that that work, set in a poor-white boarding house in Johannesburg, found a theatre (in Glasgow). Meanwhile, he returned to his single-room, two-character, 'family' format with *Hello and Goodbye*, a 'Port Elizabeth story' structured and developed more tightly than its predecessors, in two acts, and first performed at the Library Theatre, Johannesburg, in October 1965, with Fugard and Molly Seftel, directed by Barney Simon.

Hello and Goodbye is the harrowing account of a brief return home to the cramped family cottage in one of the poorer quarters of Port Elizabeth of Hester Smit, ostensibly to get her share of the money she thinks her crippled father received as compensation for an accident on the railways many years before. Once again two orphaned siblings struggle for recognition, trying to establish a coherent sense of self against the pressures of an uncertain past, remembered differently by each of them. Like Morris, Hester has returned partly out of guilt for leaving her brother; but this time it is the brother at home who has become the introspective neurotic, unable to work, crushed by Calvinist fears and imaginings. The play opens with Johnnie alone, tapping out the passage of time on the side of a glass, wondering if he is going mad as he tries to avoid contemplating his father's recent death (Fugard thought of this play as 'dedicated to his father', who died in 1961, three years before he completed it (N. 121)). The play ends with Hester's departure back to Johannesburg, after discovering – while the past of the 'second-hand Smits of Valley Road' (*PEP* 165) has been emptied onto the stage – that Johnnie misled her into thinking her father was still alive in the next room, and that there was money to fulfil her dream of changing her life.

This final disappointment provokes Hester into attacking her brother, knocking him to the floor: 'More! Explode! Swallow me up' (*PEP* 186) he exclaims, echoing the words he used to describe the explosion that mutilated her father. Hester apologizes, and urges him to leave with her: 'Get a job, a girl, have some good times' (*PEP* 187). But Johnnie remains prone until she departs; then, in a chilling conclusion, he struggles up onto his father's crutches, to assume the dead man's identity. 'Let's face it – a man on his own two legs is a shaky proposition' (*PEP* 188). We are left with the image of Johnnie facing us, uttering the final ironic word of the play as darkness descends: 'Resurrection' (*PEP* 189). Johnnie's failed rebirth suggests a wider failure to escape the distortions of faith and history underpinning apartheid. Just as Morris returns compulsively to the word of the Bible in a vain attempt to understand the 'retribution' he thinks he deserves for trying to pass as white, so Johnnie returns compulsively to his father's faith in providence to justify his own weakness in being unable to leave home. Hester, on the other hand, openly hates her father's memory, although she cannot reject everything from her past: as she pulls a dress out of one of the boxes lugged onto the stage, she recognizes her mother's smell:

> HESTER. I'm telling you, it's her. I remember. How do you like that, hey? All these years. Hell, man, it hurts.
>
> (*PEP* 160)

Her search for 'compensation' becomes a search for her childhood, and for the suppressed feelings of past family ties. But memory brings with it pain, too, and anger, as she explains to her brother the meaning of marriage: 'One man's slave all your life, slog away until you're in your grave. For what? Happiness in Heaven? I seen them – Ma and the others like them [. . .] bruises every payday.' Johnnie's version is different:

> JOHNNIE. Daddy never beat Mommie. He was never drunk.
> HESTER. Because he couldn't. He was a crock. But he did it other ways. She fell into her grave the way they all do – tired, *moeg*. Frightened! I saw her.
> JOHNNIE. This is terrible, Hester.
> HESTER. You're damned right it is. It's hell, they live in hell, but they're too frightened to do anything about it because there's always somebody around shouting God and Judgement [. . .]
>
> (*PEP* 176)

Purposely misunderstanding Johnnie's remark, Hester speaks on behalf of the silenced wives and mothers of the community – of many communities.

Hester has been said to lack agency; but she releases herself from the prison house of the past when Johnnie cannot – an achievement forcefully represented on stage by Yvonne Bryceland and Janet Suzman during the 1970s. Suzman's performance at the King's Head in London in 1973 (with Ben Kingsley, in a shortened version) trod a fine line between Hester's vulgarity and vulnerability; Bryceland's performance at the Riverside in 1978, subsequently filmed by the BBC, better expressed her courage. As a play detailing the struggle for self-recognition, *Hello and Goodbye* has a relentlessness reminiscent of Eugene O'Neill, while retaining hints of celebration. Having tested Camus's 'courageous pessimism' first with Milly (in *People Are Living There*), Fugard found it once again, at least momentarily, in Hester (*N.* 119, 127–8). Survival does not mean Hester will give up her life as a prostitute; it means that unlike her brother, she knows what she is. That is enough, apparently.

As the impact of apartheid deepened, and Fugard found himself involved in the Serpent Players' experiment, he was also turning over in his mind the complex of images that were to issue in the successor to these two Port Elizabeth Plays, *Boesman and Lena* – a play whose astonishing achievement reflects an even greater demand to witness to the wretched of the earth. The first version, with Fugard as Boesman and Bryceland as Lena, was performed at the Rhodes University Little Theatre in Grahamstown in the Eastern Cape, in July 1969, under the playwright's direction.

Like *The Blood Knot/Blood Knot* and *Hello and Goodbye*, this was a play that grew from a coincidence between Fugard's observation of the discarded people of the city, and rumination upon his own family relations – specifically, on his marriage. Yet the most immediate and lasting prompt for his imagination was a Coloured woman, seen one day in August 1965 when he was returning by car with Barney Simon and Serpent Player Mabel Magada from Cradock Magistrate's Court, where Magada's husband and fellow-Player Norman Ntshinga had been condemned to Robben Island for belonging to the ANC. About ten miles outside Cradock, Fugard noticed a woman walking beside the road, with a large bundle on her head and a shopping bag in her hand. He stopped and helped put her

37

bundle (including a bath and domestic implements) in the trunk. In tears, the woman told her story, of being

> chased off a farm after her husband's death about three days previously. She was walking to another farm where she had a friend. Later on she told us she had nine children but didn't know where they were. She thought a few of them were in P[ort].E[lizabeth].
>
> I told her to tell me when to stop. When she'd got into the car she had said she was going very far. After driving about fifteen miles it became obvious that she would never have reached her destination on foot that day. We asked her about this and she said she knew it and would have slept in one of the stormwater drains [. . .] Finally, when we reached the gate where she wanted to get off I gave her two of the three shillings left in my pocket, she cried again. I put the bundle on her head; May carried the shopping-bag down an embankment to the gate and set her on her way. My last image of her is the thin, scrawny ankles between her old shoes and the edge of her old skirt, trudging away into the bush. (*N.* 123–4)

Fugard said he would 'never escape' from the story of the woman on the road. But the question is: what did he do with it? *Boesman and Lena* certainly provides one answer. The play's generation also included other figures wandering the outskirts of the city, such as the 'coloured derelict and his wife' with their neighbour, an elderly, turbercular black man, whose shacks Fugard saw being destroyed by the authorities. To a 'Lena' spotted walking 'like a somnambulist' beside the Swartkops River just north of the city one bitterly cold July in 1968, he realized that he and his companion 'were merely "white men" '; yet her presence made a 'demand' on him: 'that the truth be told, that I must not bear false witness' (*N.* 166).

Thus *Boesman and Lena* became a conscious attempt to bear witness to the disinherited, through its focus on the lives of Coloured people thrust even further beyond the pale than the brothers of *The Blood Knot/Blood Knot*. 'Boesman' is an insulting name for someone of mixed race, implying Bushman or Khoisan descent – that is, from people once hunted down as vermin by the settlers; Lena calls herself a '*Hotnot meid*', acknowledging her equally marginalized status – or rather, subject to her partner's blows and curses, doubly marginalized. And yet, as the play reveals, there is always someone further down the scale than yourself, always somebody from whom you can try and differentiate yourself, and demand recognition: in Lena's case, an anonymous black man.

The play begins as a man and a woman, visibly Coloured down and outs, arrive beside the Swartkops River estuary, forced from their Korsten pondok by the white man's bulldozer. 'Here?' is the resonant first word of the play; a question, an interrogation of place. The two carry their world on their shoulders, in an environment more desolate than that of the brothers of *The Blood Knot/Blood Knot*: the stage is '*empty*'. As Stanley Kauffman astutely observed of the 1970 New York production, this is a play in which *the ground* is important: 'On this mud, out of which we all come, Boesman and Lena make their camp.'[10] This is almost the entire action. Except that one elderly black man comes out of the dark to share their fire, and dies beside it. The pair take up their burdens again, and move on, we know not where.

The play's minimal setting, sparse action and stripped-down dialogue suggest a limit beyond which human endurance cannot go, just as they represent an advance in Fugard's Beckettian dramaturgy. Yet, by a profound paradox, it is at this limit that the possibility of hope, of survival, even joy, emerges. The possibility arrives in a moment of performative excess when, despite herself, and all that she has suffered at the hands of the whites and her partner, Lena finds herself able to sing, to dance, to stamp down on that mud from which we all come, and to which we shall all return. Her song celebrates, as it echoes, her miserable and mean existence; her dance, an overcoming of that '*angular, gaunt cipher of poverty*' (*PEP* 193) to which her body has been reduced:

> Korsten had its empties
> Swartkops got its bait
> Lena's got her bruises
> Cause Lena's a *Hotnot meid*.
>
> Kleinskool got prickly pears
> Missionvale's got salt
> Lena's got a Boesman
> So it's always Lena's fault.

Coegakop is far away
Redhouse up the river
Lena's in the mud again
Outa's sitting with her.

(*PEP* 234)

The list of local place names reflects Lena's struggle, throughout the play, to create meaning out of her existence, and an identity for herself through the fragments of memory tied to these poor little Eastern Cape towns and villages, by discovering the order in which she and Boesman have visited them. As Errol Durbach has pointed out, the two carry with them the general memory of three centuries of racist history, as well as the specific memory of apartheid's Group Areas legislation, which uprooted people because of their inferior racial status.[11]

Yet the anti-apartheid specifics are finally less important than they might seem, although, like the preceding plays, *Boesman and Lena* revolves around the fundamental question of difference and recognition (and is the only play in which the word 'apartheid' occurs (*PEP* 233)). Lena's song ends by reminding herself that 'Outa' is sitting with her – a figure whose condition finally witnesses to the depths of depravity to which people may sink in a country rooted in racial division – when, in fearful, guilt-ridden brutality, Boesman kicks the old man's body, as Lena asks: 'How do you throw away a dead *kaffer*?' (*PEP* 240). Was it for this scene that in 1984 the Cape Department of Education ordered all copies of the play in their schools to be taken out and burned? Not at all. It was because of complaints that the language in the play was 'foul' – that is, precisely the bastardized, hence illegitimate discourse of the 'Hotnot'. Certainly the play is replete with the vulgar terms (*poep, moer*) education authorities are likely to object to, no matter how prevalent they are among the people the play is about (not to mention schoolchildren), or how carefully they are in fact stitched into the dialogue to create a moving dialect of despair. Earlier universalist readings of *Boesman and Lena* (by, for example, Vandenbroucke[12]) may have led to a presumption that the play was as safe as – Shakespeare, perhaps?

But to deny the specific, historical dimension of Fugard's work is to render it naive. Equally naive would be to suggest

40

that the play was simply an attack upon apartheid legislation, although, without its originating context of forced removals, the struggles of Boesman and Lena would be less significant. Language, like location, involves a communal, or at least joint act – something that, from the start, these two fight to achieve, despite having internalized the ideology of difference in both race and gender terms: 'He's not brown people, he's black people,' Boesman says of Outa; Lena refers to the man's 'baboon language' (*PEP* 212). But Outa, who cannot speak or understand their language, learns Lena's name, thereby acknowledging her existence. While representing the silenced, suffering indigene, he gives Lena a sense of self: she asks the old man to be her 'witness', to 'listen' as she tells her tale (*PEP* 214, 216, 217). If in death the man seems to pose a threat, he had briefly become someone to witness her sufferings at the hands of her partner as well as the white man, those remembered miscarriages in the dark, when her pain was 'a candle *entjie* [stump] and a donkey's face' (*PEP* 219) – an image recalling the Christian birth scene, elaborated by some critics into a belief in transcendence on the basis of Fugard's Notebook entry about the 'metaphysical' dimension of the couple's predicament (*N.* 168) – a predicament from which, however, Outa remains excluded.

The play also prompted much self-questioning on Fugard's part. Did it, he worried, reveal him unable to align himself with the wished-for future of his country, 'a possibility, in which I believe but of which I have no clear image? My failure of imagination?' (*N.* 178–81).[13] But who, after all, was able to imagine the future in 1968? And if, as a liberal, Fugard was unable to align himself with the forces of resistance, this inability shrinks into insignificance beside the play's achievement: articulating the grounds for such resistance with unignorable force when squatters, refugees and 'asylum-seekers' still roam the landscapes of the world with their meagre belongings, searching for a place, a home.

Ironically, the play to which a charge of imaginative insufficiency might more justifiably be levelled, *A Lesson from Aloes* (1978), was more explicitly connected with its times. The play examined the options open to those who resisted: departure into exile, as chosen by Steve Daniels, the Coloured activist who has been betrayed; or a dogged sitting-out of the troubles, as chosen by Afrikaner Piet Bezuidenhout, who tells his English wife Gladys that, if his involvement in the Port Elizabeth bus boycotts was useless, there is still the 'lesson' that 'An evil system isn't a natural disaster. There's nothing you can do to stop a drought, but bad laws and social injustice are man-made and can be unmade by men. It's as simple as that' (*IP* 242). Of course it is not; and by the end Piet is left contemplating his beloved aloes, still under suspicion of having betrayed his comrades (an earlier title for the play was 'The Informer'); while Steve leaves for England on a one-way exit permit, having been broken by interrogation; and Gladys, for whom 'politics' and 'the black man's misery' don't make 'the only victims' (*IP* 267), and who has been violated by the police removal of her intimate diaries, prepares to return to Fort England mental hospital. The play, set in the 1960s, registers the pessimism and confusion of the period immediately after the vicious crushing of the Soweto Rising of 1976, two years before its first performance at the Market Theatre.

A Lesson from Aloes is best thought of as psychological rather than social-realist drama, the detailed textures of its lower-middle-class, predominantly Afrikaans, Algoa Park location notwithstanding. Despite local enthusiasm for the Market production, and the New York Drama Critics' Circle Award as the best play of the 1980–1 season on Broadway, its reception was mixed. The play took Fugard back into the past, its mood of paralysis suggesting an inability to face the present, much less contemplate the future. Other 'white liberal' writers of the time, from Nadine Gordimer to J. M. Coetzee, were turning away from realism with more profound results – as in Gordimer's *The Conservationist* (1974) and Coetzee's *In the Heart of the Country* (1976), both uncovering radical new ways of exploring the inner life in reaction to external events. Doubtless the novel form offers more scope for the articulation of the inner consciousness and memory, although Fugard managed to delve even further into his personal past with a play that marked a turning point, *'Master Harold' . . . and the Boys* (1982), even more precisely located in the Port Elizabeth the playwright knew, with his mother's tearoom in St George's Park as its setting, and urging confessional and intimate revelation as its *raison d'être* – bearing witness, so to speak, to his own past, rather than the present of others. In this sense it belongs with his more 'interior' plays, such as *Valley Song* (1995) and *The Captain's Tiger* (1998), which ultimately engage audiences with his own position, rather than with the demands of the disinherited.

The move inwards might seem a failure on Fugard's part, echoing the failure of the English-language liberal tradition fully to acknowledge the voiceless, even as it gestures towards their presence. Yet we must recall that, as Fugard pursued his personal trajectory – encouraged by growing acclaim world-wide – he had already entered into the extraordinary, collab-orative theatrework that was to issue in the 'Township Plays'.

3

Township Witnessing

In 1986 the exiled ANC activist-poet Mongane Wally Serote pointed out that, among the various art forms then emerging from South Africa, it was theatre that had shown the most impressive potential, and, in particular, the form of 'workshop theatre' introduced by Athol Fugard, John Kani and Winston Ntshona, through productions such as *The Coat, Sizwe Bansi Is Dead*, and *The Island*. Serote also included *The Blood Knot/Blood Knot*, which, although not part of the same group of plays, similarly represented a trangressive urge: to cross the racial divide so as to ensure that performers created a representation of themselves and their lives that effectively challenged the status quo. Theatre, stated Serote, had become a reflection of 'the struggle'.[1]

In retrospect, this seems an exaggeration, characteristic of its time. Nevertheless, it is important to recall that the small-scale, often experimental theatrework with Fugard and performers from the townships did constitute an alternative form of dissent during the darkest decades of the apartheid regime, when the liberation movements were banned or dispersed, and censorship was at its most severe. There were other groups across the lines: Rob McLaren's Workshop '71 in Johannesburg, Rob Amato's Imitha Players in East London, Don Maclennan's Ikwezi Players in Grahamstown. But Fugard's work with the Serpent Players was earlier, and their example led to more profound and lasting results. It was the experience of seeing *Sizwe Bansi Is Dead* while a factory worker in Empangeni in 1976 that set Mbongeni Ngema on the road to *Woza Albert!* (1981) and the hugely successful township productions *Asinamali!* (1986) and *Sarafina!* (1987).[2] These works incorporated 1970s Black Consciousness symbolism while providing their star performers with a temporary escape from apartheid; they represented popular attempts to create meaning out of the everyday lives of those struggling to survive, speaking on behalf of those such as the students of Morris Isaacson High School, who led the Soweto Rising of 1976, and whose experiences formed the basis of *Sarafina!*

Yet Fugard's group went beyond other South African playmakers to make a daring claim: that theatre counts in the most extreme circumstances, such as those that prevailed upon Robben Island. Ironically, since 1997, when the hated top-security prison became a national museum and heritage centre, complete with ex-prisoner tourist guides, it has not been easy to remember those conditions in detail. Entering the prison's narrow, high-windowed recreation room nowadays, it is – as I found on a recent visit – sometimes forgotten that plays such as Sophocles' fifth-century tragedy *Antigone* (with Mandela as King Creon) were once put on there before officials, guards and prisoners. As Milan Kundera once remarked, 'the struggle of man against power is the struggle of memory against forgetting'.[3] Performing plays like *The Island* is part of *that* struggle, which includes recalling how such plays came about, as well as what their immediate and long-term effects have been. In the 'post-apartheid' era, too much of the past remains potent, as the Truth and Reconciliation Commission (TRC) has demonstrated, for the Fugardian contribution to be dismissed or erased.

Fugard's impulse to represent those of his compatriots disinherited or oppressed by society appears from very early on in his career. On 18 June 1954, for example, an article by an unknown freelance reporter appeared before the predominantly white readership of the Port Elizabeth *Evening Post*, entitled 'Drama of P.E.'s Night School for Adults', explaining why '500 African men and women of all ages attend the night school in New Brighton'. It engaged readers' sympathies by dramatizing the stories of individuals such as 'Philip' and 'Lena'. For men like Philip, learning to write a letter home meant some alleviation of the loneliness of urban life; while for women like Lena, learning to read meant buying an occasional tin of 'something special' for her children. The author was Fugard, intent on representing to the powerful the everyday experiences, indeed the lives, of those so much less powerful than they.

This triangular relationship, the playwright representing the 'other' to others, brings difficulties – even when working directly with those whose lives he is trying to represent and, at times, finding audiences who share their experiences. What is not in doubt is Fugard's aim to bear witness, however problematic the results. We have seen how this aim came to be expressed in Lena's testimony; it had already begun with representations of black township life in his first full-length plays, *No-Good Friday* (1958), and *Nongogo* (1959). These apprentice plays arose out of his encounter with Sophiatown, while it was still possible for whites to enter freely (permits were subsequently required for any designated 'black' area). A unique part of Johannesburg in which black people had freehold rights, the township was destroyed by the implementation of the Group Areas Act during the late 1950s, and its 60,000 inhabitants transported to what was to become Soweto (South Western Townships). It had been 'the most lively, important and sophisticated' of black townships; in its 'crowded and narrow streets walked philosophers and gangsters, musicians and pick-pockets, short-story writers and businessmen'; it embodied 'all that was best and worst of African life in towns'.[4]

Both the best and worst of township life appear in *No-Good Friday*, which opens in a 1950s Sophiatown backyard, late one Friday afternoon, as a young woman takes down the washing, and sounds offstage indicate the bustle of others preparing for the return of wage-earners with their pay packets – or tales of woe, such as that recounted by Guy, the saxophonist, whose entry initiates the action, and whose music punctuates it throughout. He tells Rebecca of a futile search for employment in 'Goli' (the City of Gold, Johannesburg), before their conversation shifts to Rebecca's man Willie, in his 'First year BA . . . Correspondent', whose aim thereby is to become 'independent'. 'A big word, isn't it?' she remarks bitterly. 'He just doesn't need anyone.' But, counters Guy, 'you can't always add up on paper what a man needs, like your instalments on the stove each month' (*TP* 6–7). The homely, proverbial image anticipates the main point of the play: Willie's needs exceed

46

what any of them foresee, and constitute his tragedy. Fugard uses the backyard setting structurally and visually as a frame within which to develop the interior, domestic scenes, thereby reinforcing the play's message – that their environment is crushing the characters' private hopes and desires.

This is the typical perspective of naturalistic drama; but the impact upon the playwright of engaging with his chosen performers – by writing draft scenes and then having them improvised upon – infused the work with a more than merely social-documentary tone. When the white missionary, Father Higgins (based on Trevor Huddleston and played by Fugard), brings in the pathetic, dazed figure of Tobias, wrapped in his rural blanket, in stark contrast to the jazzy, 'American' clothes of the others, Willie exclaims:

WILLIE. Why do they do it!
HIGGINS. Do what?
WILLIE. That! Why do they come here, like that!
HIGGINS. He only wants to live, Willie.

(*TP* 11)

Tobias's innocent desire to better his conditions leads to Willie's final, futile stand against the tsotsi (gangster) Shark, who murders Tobias as a warning to those who do not pay protection money. Tobias represents the peasant farmworker drawn to the city by incomprehensible and irresistible forces, a dynamic given a specifically South African twist by the apartheid system, which defined people like him as 'surplus' labour to be left or dumped in the 'reserves' (subsequently Bantustans/Homelands).

But Tobias's characterization reveals the difficulty of attempting to represent the problems of another with less than full knowledge, or without the openness to it that Fugard later found with the Serpent Players. When the man composes a letter to his wife (anticipating Sizwe Bansi's monologue), it is in the stereotypical and condescendingly naive 'Jim comes to Jo'burg' language of earlier, well-intentioned liberal works such as Alan Paton's *Cry, the Beloved Country* (1948). The playwright's own concerns become evident after Tobias's murder at the end of scene 2, when the focus shifts to an account of Willie's tortures of conscience, rather than how the community might deal with the murder. Willie, like his creator, is at odds with his environment, struggling vainly to be the conscience of others. Nevertheless, *No-Good Friday* helped legitimize the aspirations of the township-dwellers it represented, and began to create the space Fugard was to exploit more effectively later. *No-Good Friday* had its premiere on 30 August 1958 on the stage of the Bantu Men's Social Centre in Johannesburg, the kind of limited, all-purpose venue made available for the black elite since the 1930s, when the Bantu Dramatic Society was set up to perform African drama – although apart from H. I. E. Dhlomo's turgid if well-meaning historical plays, they put on mainly European classics. *No-Good Friday* attracted sufficient attention to transfer briefly to the Brian Brooke Theatre – an all-white venue in which the multi-talented Lewis Nkosi substituted for Fugard as Father Higgins, since Brooke forbade a 'mixed' cast. The 'critical European audience thundered with applause' according to the popular black monthly *Zonk*, which praised Fugard for giving his unknown actors the opportunity to show their talents, as well as for revealing 'a great understanding of the African people and their way of life'.[5]

Fugard's involvement in township cultural activity can be seen as part of a larger movement by liberal whites during the 1950s to exploit the talents of black people – the most influential result of which was the African musical *King Kong* (1950), produced, scripted and directed by whites, but using black singers, actors and musicians. This form of cultural interaction led to a series of glossily packaged 'African' musicals and plays produced with the blessing of the authorities, since they offered white audiences at home and abroad an acceptable image of blacks. What Fugard and his township collaborators provided was different in scale and ambition, although race barriers nonetheless generated tension. When Bloke Modisane was approached by the Fugards 'with a bottle of brandy' and a request to play Shark, he agreed, but called the all-black Brooke production of *No-Good Friday* a 'betrayal', saying he and the others had 'relented' to Brooke only because it meant so much to Fugard.[6]

According to Fugard, the 'Sophiatown group' included 'one splendid actor in the person of Zakes Mokae', who played one of Shark's murderous sidekicks in *No-Good Friday* so well that the more substantial part of Blackie was created for him in *Nongogo*. Meeting Mokae was the start of 'one of the really rich working relationships of my life', said Fugard.[7] Mokae, like the rest of the group, had no dramatic training, and his stage experience was limited to playing the saxophone for Trevor Huddleston's jazz band. But he was the first performer to inspire Fugard into writing directly for him, as the subsequent creation of *The Blood Knot/Blood Knot* showed. Crucially, the number of characters was halved for Fugard's second 'township' play, and the setting, Queeny's shebeen, stayed the same throughout the twenty-four hours of the action. Narrowing down his focus, Fugard was discovering the kind of drama he would do best – economical, intense and unified. Much of the two-act play consists of a two-hander between Queeny, the middle-aged former 'Nongogo' or mineworkers' prostitute of the title, and the young salesman Johnny, who vainly hopes to make her part of his newly 'respectable' life. *Nongogo* was first produced in the Bantu Men's Social Centre, before transferring to a church basement, where it could be staged in the round.

The central conflict of the play, between two people whose images of each other fail to coincide with reality, was to become a familiar Fugardian theme. At first the play seemed as much in the 'tough neorealism' mode as its predecessor,[8] its shebeen ambience almost lovingly recreated by later productions, such as Lucille Gillwald's influential 1981 version at the Laager studio in the Market, for which director and cast researched the lives of the still-active shebeen queens of Johannesburg to make it more 'authentic'. But, as with the first production, there were complaints of distortion and exaggeration from black audiences, who were particularly provoked by the final scene, when Queeny reveals her past as a 'mineworker's whore' to Johnny – a highly theatrical moment, even – Lewis Nkosi observed – 'deeply stirring', but, as he went on, it did not arise 'out of *our* social experience'.[9] Thus it seems like Fugard speaking when Johnny reflects, after confessing to a secret as 'filthy' as Queeny's (he has been sodomized in one of the all-male compounds): 'sometimes I get the crazy idea that a man can change the world he lives in. Hell! You can't even change yourself' (*TP* 113). Yet, if the

49

playwright manipulates these black characters to test his own sense of individual futility, he thereby touches a deeper truth: that the sexual exploitation that has blasted the hopes of both Queeny and Johnny has a common source in the gold mines. The centrality of the mines to the structure of the economy was to be highlighted by Witwatersrand University's History Workshop, whose research informed the work of the Junction Avenue Theatre Company – their *Sophiatown* (1986) was set in the same period as Fugard's first two plays, and it expressed the same urge to represent the lives of ordinary township-dwellers, although their work also revealed the ambiguous value of invoking the memory of those almost pre-apartheid days – appearing to celebrate the poverty they represented.

Fugard was able to confront and overcome this danger in his work with the Serpent Players. What they celebrated was survival, and a new kind of hybrid witnessing, a mix of Brecht's didacticism and Grotowski's physicality, on the one hand, and black urban narrative performance traditions, on the other. The originating moment occurred when Fugard was approached by the New Brighton group in 1963. The enthusiasm and gratitude of the original members towards their mentor are undeniable; ten years later, when John Kani and Winston Ntshona began to tour the world, they insisted that the initiative and creativity had come from their side. But both sides needed the different kinds of creativity each could bring, a mutual engagement that challenged the laws and customs of their divided society. It is too easy for critics to attack – as they have – Fugard's motives. Rob MacLaren quotes Steve Biko asking: 'How many white people fighting for their version of change in South Africa are really motivated by genuine concern and not by guilt?' But what really matters far more than the extent of Fugard's guilt, shared no doubt by many at home and abroad, is what he did as a result.[10]

This was to commit himself to working with the Serpent Players, at no small personal cost, and under police surveillance (his passport was revoked for four years). To begin with, under his expert guidance, the Players performed cheaply mounted township versions of European classics, notably a popular production of Machiavelli's hilarious *Mandragola* re-titled *The Cure* (1963). But a clamp-down on the Eastern Cape made them look for ways of using the actors' own experiences as the basis for their productions. When one of the Players was arrested in December 1964, shortly before the opening of their version of Brecht's *Caucasian Chalk Circle*, it was the beginning of a new and radical phase. The coat of a man who had just been sentenced on a trumped-up political charge became the 'mandate' for the first reworking of their own experiences – in *The Coat*, an 'Acting Exercise' that combined narratives of their lives with Brechtian estrangement techniques. A presenter began the play by addressing the white, self-styled 'theatre-appreciation' audience for whom it was was first performed on 28 November 1966 with these words:

> New Brighton. I often wonder what that name means to outsiders, like you. I am using the word in its purely descriptive sense – we live inside and you live outside. That world where your servants go at the end of the day, that ugly scab of pondokkies [shacks] and squalor that spoils the approach to Port Elizabeth. If you are interested in knowing something about it we might be able to help you, because we accepted the chance to come here tonight so that we could tell you about a coat, a man's coat, which came back to New Brighton in a stranger's shopping bag. (*TP* 123)

The performers, among them John Kani, introduced themselves using the names of characters they had played in previous Serpent productions, so as to hide their identities from the security police, as well as to direct attention towards the conditions of their lives, rather than merely evoke sympathy.

In fact the white Port Elizabeth audience, who had asked to see a sample of the Players' work, sat frozen 'in horror and fascination' as the daily oppressions of their New Brighton neighbours were enacted. Fugard's aim to 'shatter white complacency and its conspiracy of silence' was fulfilled, at least within the confines of the occasion. The group was aware of the risks – their performance (in a church hall) was permitted by the authorities only if the actors did not use the hall toilets and returned to the township immediately afterwards – and only after much argument did they proceed, as an 'act of solidarity'.[11] From then on, the Players alternated between European classics and improvisations on township themes in similar unofficial venues, which Fugard was increasingly prevented from attending – while he went on writing and directing *Hello and Goodbye, People Are Living There* and *Boesman and Lena*. This almost schizoid existence came to a head in 1972–3 with the creation of two of the greatest works associated with his name: *Sizwe Bansi Is Dead* and *The Island*, devised jointly with two of the most talented and disciplined Serpent Players, John Kani and Winston Ntshona.

In 1972, after performing together in a hugely successful production of Camus's *The Just* (retitled *The Terrorists*) at the Space Theatre in Cape Town, Kani and Ntshona had made a momentous decision – to become full-time actors. It was not a recognized profession for blacks, and so they had to be classified in their passbooks as Fugard's domestic servants. Within months of the decision, their joint commitment generated the workshop productions of *Sizwe Bansi* and *The Island*. According to Kani, Fugard and the two actors had been looking for a two-hander based on urban black experience; they finally found their mandate in a photograph of a smiling black man – who, they agreed, would smile like that only if his passbook was in order. This led to a play in which the central character, played by Ntshona as rural migrant Sizwe Bansi, assumes the identity of a dead man (Robert Zwelinzima), by taking on his passbook, so as to continue working in Port Elizabeth without harassment – although not for ever. 'A black man stay out of trouble? Impossible', as he tells his friend Buntu (Kani). 'Our skin is trouble' (*TP* 191).

The choice of actors, of acting as a means for survival, as well as the physical immediacy of the action, provided a unique challenge to performers as well as audiences – who had to cope with moments such as that when the drunken Robert/Sizwe, his mouth messily smeared with the remains of an orange, drops his trousers to grip his genitals and exclaim 'Look at me! I'm a man. I've got legs. I can run with a wheelbarrow full of cement! I'm strong! I'm a man. Look! I've got a wife. I've got four children. How many has he made, lady? [*The man sitting next to her.*] Is he a man? What has he got that I haven't?' (*TP* 182). Simple and direct, deliberately shocking, such moments packed a profound punch, undermining racial (if not gender) stereotyping, while viewers some-

52

times shrank in embarassment before a demand for dignity and recognition made thereby all the stronger and more memorable.

Never was the potential of artistic hybridity, of Grotowskian 'poor theatre' in an African context, more convincingly embodied. Grotowski's views on theatre chime closely with Fugard's: always aiming towards a 'pure' theatre experience, without make-up, scenery, lighting, sound, or even costume, to enable the actor to communicate as directly as possible, which involves schooling a dedicated troupe of performers disciplining themselves physically and mentally to the extent that what they create experientially on stage 'resonates' with their audience on an almost unconscious, subtextual level. Fugard had already registered the impact of the influential Polish director's emphasis upon the 'creative' as opposed to the merely 'illustrative' use of actors in his 1971 *Orestes* project. This method enabled him to push his team beyond the lack of ambiguity about mere 'facts', towards exploring the witnessing potential of images such as that of the smiling black man that provoked *Sizwe Bansi* – a play whose action hinges upon a photo-flash, a freeze-frame of Robert/Sizwe/Ntshona striding towards the photographer Styles/Kani as he strides simultaneously towards the audience, taking us into the subtextual dimension in which he delivers his 'story' of taking on a new identity.

The play revolves around a series of such oral narratives within narratives, cleverly transporting audiences into the multiple perspectives of its characters from the start. After engaging our sympathies by reading out the day's headlines from a newspaper (altered according to the time of production), a dapper young man recalls the day the workers were preparing for a visit by 'Mr Henry Ford Junior Number Two' at the Ford plant in Port Elizabeth (where Kani himself once worked). The panic among the white bosses, their commands that result in a furious sweeping, washing and painting, and the black man's role as translator of his white foreman's words, telling workers to smile while they work – all this is re-enacted in energetic, hilarious and socio-politically significant detail. But, when Styles impersonates his own former self at the Ford assembly plant, he shows how subservience is a role that

53

masks the workers' sense of their own identity, their inner resistance to appropriation. 'Tell the boys in your language, that this is a very big day,' the white boss instructs. Styles quotes himself 'translating' that day:

> 'Gentlemen, the old fool says this is a hell of a big day in our lives.'
> The men laughed.
> 'Tell the boys that Mr Henry Ford the Second, the owner of this place, is going to visit us. Tell them Mr Ford is the big Baas [. . .] a Makulu baas.' [. . .]
> 'Mr "Baas" Bradley says [. . .] Mr Ford is the grandmother baas of them all.' (TP 153)

The climax of the sequence arrives when Styles mimes how Mr Ford Number Two walked in and straight out again, demonstrating just how unimportant all these South Africans were to the real boss, and to his global company.

One of the most telling images generated by the workshop was that used by Styles/Kani when recounting his experiences of running the tiny photographer's studio that he called 'a strong-room of dreams' – the dreamers being 'My people. The simple people, who you never find mentioned in the history books, who never get statues erected to them, or monuments commemorating their great deeds' (TP 159). As in Brecht's 'Fragen eines lesenden Arbeiters' (Questions from a Worker who Reads), the play's concern is not for the great men who make history; its concern, which becomes the audience's concern, is for the anonymous, little people whose hopes and desires are movingly and comically represented onstage, as 'snaps' of old folk and children.

This is a radical, democratic conception of the theatre's role, defined in terms of the reproduction of images as a self-conscious process. Ironically, it is the studio in which 'dom' pass photos are taken to insert people into the bureacratic machinery of the state, which becomes the means for them to tell their stories, of life outside. Yet if *Sizwe Bansi* seems to define the achievement of Fugard and his colleagues in creative collaboration, it also suggests a limitation to their kind of theatre. Kani's and Ntshona's electrifying performances made *Sizwe Bansi* testify to the dreams of escaping the brutal and dehumanizing conditions of life for black people in South

Africa, while obscuring the danger of relying on specific performances for such testimony – and the further peril that, if we are taken today into such a 'strong-room of dreams', we may forget what we leave outside, the changing world in which new issues have emerged – such as those highlighted by the TRC, concerning how to deal with the past.

Nevertheless, local white and overseas audiences were made to witness the process of witnessing, a process taken to another socio-political level in the 1990s by the TRC. Fugard testifies to the testimony of others, the experiences of black people like Kani and Ntshona, although not necessarily the experiences of the actors themselves. This is a central paradox, developed further in the succeeding play, *The Island*, when the two actors use their own names, while neither had personally experienced the imprisonment they represented, although relatives (Kani's brother) and friends (especially members of the Serpent Players on Robben Island) had. Dori Laub refers to the process of testifying to historic trauma as 'a ceaseless struggle' that involves three distinct levels of witnessing: the level of 'being a witness oneself', the level of being involved 'not in the events, but in the account given of them', and the level 'in which the process of witnessing is itself being witnessed', a process conveying the sense of a long submerged truth that has become 'an elusive memory' needing to be recovered.[12]

This latter level is the sense in which plays such as these have the potential to continue bearing witness, if only partially and with the connivance or collusion of audiences – such as the 1974 New Brighton audience who took witnessing to a place no white audience could. As Fugard observed, 'It is one thing to try to educate a comfortable white audience into what the deeply hated Reference [pass] Book means to a black man and something else to confront, and in a sense challenge, an angry black audience with those same realities.'[13] The 1974 township audience was likely to be angry because of the recent wave of detentions, mostly of young student leaders whose militancy was to explode in the 1976 Soweto Rising. The performance began with a Brechtian announcer warning they were in for 'straight theatre', without music, women or dancing; but, far from producing anger, the play soon had its audience roaring with laughter – until the moment when

Buntu/Kani switched the photographs in the passbooks. At first Sizwe rejects the idea of the switch, as it means abandoning his name; but, before Ntshona could make his objection, the audience, which had fallen silent during the first few seconds of the operation, erupted: 'Don't do it brother! You'll land in trouble!' 'To hell with it. Go ahead and try. They haven't caught me yet.' The performance was halted as the action of the audience overtook the action of the play; and the evening concluded with a singing of the banned ANC anthem – while the security police stayed outside.[14]

Such a response to the play is inconceivable nowadays, yet its subversive potential remains strong, and extends beyond the place as well as the time of its creation – as was demonstrated, for example, by the Arabic Al-Kasaba Theatre production (shown at the London International Festival of Theatre at the Royal Court 23–5 June 1997), which used the *Sizwe Bansi* plot to articulate the sufferings of two Palestinian workers seeking employment in Israel. Incorporating the political present into an image of past resistance is itself the subject of *The Island*, which, for all its brilliant distillation of black political prisoners' experience into a multidimensional symbol, as the two men enact their version of the ancient Greek drama of *Antigone* on Robben Island, inevitably lacks some of the everyday humour of its immediate predecessor, *Sizwe Bansi*. But then, as George Steiner has well put it, *The Island* is 'the satyr play to all preceding "Antigones" ';[15] and, I would add, its harshness breaks open the whole Western liberal humanist tradition, which silences resistance in order to maintain a 'balance' of voices.

Thus, unlike the comic, almost music-hall opening of *Sizwe Bansi*, *The Island* begins with a harrowing image of ceaseless labour, as two men mime the digging of sand at one end of the stage, filling a wheelbarrow, pushing it to the other end and emptying it. The pointless monotony of imprisonment, the Sisyphean absurdity of life in gaol, is enforced by making this dumb show last a good ten minutes in the theatre. The real sweat and pain of the actors were offered as a testimony to the suffering of their brothers on Robben Island, a point reinforced by the 1985 revival in Cape Town during the State of Emergency, when Kani and Ntshona publicly declared that every performance was 'an endorsement of the local and international call' for the immediate release of 'all political prisoners and detainees'.[16] But now that these prisoners have been released, what can the play call on? Does it become the 'universal', 'metaphysical' drama that many – at the time and later – have called it?

Like all great drama, *The Island* transcends itself, as it transcends the immediate circumstances of its making, and creates suggestive links with other times and places, other situations of tyranny. But that is not the same as saying that it is 'transcendent', much less universal. As John Kani remarked at the time, 'The truth is bigger than ourselves and we should tell [our story] as simply as possible.'[17] That story climaxes after Winston as Antigone pleads guilty according to state law, then tears off his Greek disguise to go to his 'living death' unrepentant. In Sophocles' *Antigone* (the events of which are neatly summarized at the opening of scene 4), the protagonist has killed herself by the end of the play, and so no longer poses any threat to King Creon or the laws of the state; this version ends before the tragic development of the original and its cathartic resolution, leaving us with a concluding image that echoes the opening, of two men shackled together again, running, as the siren wails and darkness descends. This allows for a recognition of that brotherhood in suffering that is a consistent motif throughout, and of the men's strength against the common foe. On the spectrum of possible interpretations, you may certainly find the view that this is at best a passive position, accepting the power of the state for all its imperfections, and some have seen *The Island* in this way; I am more convinced every time I watch it in the theatre that the concluding image, which reminds us of the men helping each other at the beginning, anticipates that solidarity in suffering that eventually overcame their captors, as it helped to overcome the apartheid tyranny in fact.

Unlike well-meaning, but drearily one-dimensional 'protest' theatre, the resonant, lasting qualities of Fugard's, Kani's and Ntshona's collaborative work – despite its emphasis upon urban, male experience, and despite Fugard's own different experience as a privileged white onlooker – bears witness to an understanding beyond the location or gender of its characters and performers. In any case, the lack of access for black township-dwellers then (and now) to the means of articulating their experiences makes cautious distinctions of theoretical debate about representation seem beside the point. Although of course the prime *political* aim in the long run must be for people to speak on their own behalf, this should not exclude any artist from attempting to represent those who are mute.

Many radical and dissident South Africans at home and abroad during the 1970s and 1980s shared a view of the theatre as a weapon in the class struggle, a view that dominated much alternative or oppositional theatre-making at the time, such as that produced by Maishe Maponya's Bahumutsi Players (for example, most tellingly, in *The Hungry Earth*, (Soweto, 1979)). But, as Brecht recognized, the value and extent of such 'interventionary' work depend upon the immediate theatrical and cultural context, itself an aspect of historical change and process. Thus it is not enough to say, as one might about *Sizwe Bansi Is Dead* or *The Island*, that they show how Fugard's work once bore witness, and therefore had a value, of a limited, historical kind – although that is true. This is like saying, as the reviewer of a 1995 production of *The Island* in Cape Town said, that the play shows 'protest' turned safely into 'history'.[18] But history is never safe, because it is always open to revision. And *The Island* was never simply a 'protest' play – although its protest element led to attack when it first appeared, and until the transformation of the country and the release of political prisoners. Probably no single play from South Africa has had so powerful an impact upon international opinion. Yet its basic structural dynamic, as a work drawing on the Antigone myth to expose the wider dilemma of private versus public morality, has always laid it open to criticism from those who find in it merely a reflection of passive suffering, rather than a call to arms.

But if, as I would argue, *The Island* did bear witness, rather than articulate a call to arms, then I would also argue that it continues to do so – not because things have stayed the same, but because they have changed. Nobody gets detained on Robben Island any more; and the draconian laws that led to imprisonment for dissent have been repealed. But the extreme experience to which the play testifies, and the way in which the prisoners resist and survive if only temporarily by play acting, has not dated, in a world in which the experience of being detained and tortured for one's racial identity remains depressingly familiar. The emphasis of the play upon identity – a continuation in another key of *Sizwe Bansi*'s main theme – highlights this potential. Robert Zwelinzima may act his way out of trouble as he takes on a new identity, in *Sizwe Bansi*, but 'John' and 'Winston' are already in the deepest trouble, so what they can do is perform their resistance to imprisonment by taking on apparently innocuous, 'classical' identities. This they do so as to call into question the power relations they enact at the beginning, when they run under the command of the unseen Hodoshe (a Xhosa nickname, meaning carrion fly, for a notorious warder, whose work team, 'Die Hodoshe Span', was the original, intentionally obscure title of the unscripted play).

Although *The Island* ends with the two men shackled together, running under Hodoshe's command, by then 'Winston' has articulated his claim upon a dimension of justice, which subverts that argued for by Creon as the benevolent 'father' and protector of the state. Visibly going beyond the adopted role that enabled him to oppose Creon, by '*Tearing off his wig and confronting the audience as Winston, not Antigone*', Winston exclaims

Gods of our Fathers! My Land! My Home!
Time waits no longer. I go now to my living death, because I honoured those things to which honour belongs. (*TP* 227)

Almost intolerably moving, the whole of the last scene of the four-scene drama is a play within a play: a situation the audience has been prepared for by a series of mini-narratives, beginning with the 'News Bulletin' that transforms running in the quarry into 'Black Domination was chased by White Domination' (*TP* 196), and going on to the more extended, humorous sequence when the two men recreate the conditions in Sky's shebeen at home in New Brighton (*TP* 204–6). The purpose of these sequences is twofold: they reinforce the refrain 'Nyana we Sizwe' (Xhosa: Brother of the Land) as the men repeatedly commit themselves to defiant brotherhood (most poignantly necessary when they learn John's sentence is remitted); and they prepare the audience to accept that this kind of theatre goes beyond performers merely taking on false identities; it is a kind of existential drama in which the performers are performing themselves in an act of witnessing.

The audience's reactions have been anticipated by the scene in which Winston first puts on Antigone's wig and padding (made from bits of rope, as the Serpent Players made their theatre out of whatever was to hand) and John's reaction is to fall about laughing. 'You call laughing at me, Theatre?' the big man exclaims, resentfully. 'Who cares,' comes the reply. 'As long as they' (John sweeps his arm to include both imaginary and real audiences) 'as long as they listen at the end' (*TP* 208–10). And we do, despite the clumsy, grotesque appearance of a cross-dressed prisoner playing the role he first thinks of as an emasculation, merely completing what the authorities have done to him. The audience is addressed as if we were the warders and prisoners ourselves, ensuring that we understand the link between fiction and reality, legend and history – and between memory and forgetting. It is not always noticed that the real extreme to which the men on the island can be reduced is suggested by 'old Harry', the 70-year-old prisoner who 'loves stone': 'That's why they're nice to him. He's forgotten himself. He's forgotten everything . . . why he's here, where he comes from' (*TP* 221). That is the greatest danger, which the reappearance of *The Island* helps to resist.

In considering the lasting qualities of a play, we should always consider the changing impact upon different audiences in their changing circumstances. This is even more obvious when you consider Fugard's work, and not just when a specific law engaged by one of his plays has changed, such as the laws that put men on Robben Island, or the pass laws of *Sizwe Bansi*, or the Immorality Act of *Statements after an Arrest*. Most of Fugard's plays did not touch explicitly upon the country's race laws. They strove to bear witness to what he described as 'the nameless and destitute' of his 'little corner of the world', which must mean *all* those excluded by the structures of his society. Less explicit than the work of contemporaries such as Zakes Mda, far from revolutionary, his work however tempts us to resite the boundaries of critical and theoretical discourse, so as to reinstate the more private, interior domain sidelined by the liberatory politics of the last decades of apartheid – and memory is the key: a function of both public and private understanding.

4

Carnal Realities

It is tempting to take Fugard's most successful excursions into radical play making with the Serpent Players as paradigmatic: here is a playwright who seems to have gone as far as he could in bearing witness to the demands of the oppressed black majority of his country – in current critical terminology, making a space for the voice of the other, while challenging the denial of the other underpinning apartheid. Yet at the same time as transgressing race and class boundaries to create a radical new theatre engaging with the realities of township life, the playwright was probing the inner realities of the South African psyche, most notably in the play that accompanied *Sizwe Bansi* and *The Island* in the Royal Court's 'South African Season' in 1973–4, *Statements after an Arrest under the Immorality Act*, but also in the semi-allegorical, Yeatsian *Dimetos* (1975), which followed soon after – very personal works, to which his own commitment has been lasting, sometimes in the face of severe criticism.

Thus Fugard has insisted that the *Statements* play was, out of the three that included *Sizwe Bansi* and *The Island*, the one in which he believed the most, and that would survive the longest. He said something similar about *Dimetos*: in a letter sent just days after the June 1976 Soweto Rising, he referred to the 'tidal wave of critical insensitivity and stupidity that has swept *Dimetos* away into the upper reaches of commercial Disaster', while asserting that his 'faith in the play, in the direction it has given my life and work, is total'. Twenty years later he confessed that he still felt *Dimetos* was 'standing in the wings, waiting for its moment'.[1] Is this faith misplaced, the delusion of an artist who, like Dimetos himself, has lost his way by forgetting the demands of the other? Black Consciousness leader Fatima Meer thought so: writing to Fugard from prison to ask how, after *Sizwe Bansi* and *The Island*, he could involve himself in work 'so totally without political commitment and therefore valueless in terms of the urgent and violent realities of our time?', she prompted Fugard's admission that, with *Dimetos*, he was 'finished as a committed political writer'. On the other hand, to Fugard that play was 'a profound personal statement using inner specifics in defining the condition of modern man'; telling the story of 'one man's hell' was a 'long-term investment'; it did not, it *could* not, offer the 'immediate returns' of a 'political pamphlet' (N. 223).[2]

Immediate return or long-term investment? Such stark alternatives reflect the Manichean aesthetics of the time. During the 1970s and 1980s writers such as J. M. Coetzee were finding themselves driven towards explorations of the inner world to define the condition of the white settler, if not of 'modern man'; while others, such as the Soweto poets, were expressing anger and outrage at the circumstances and beliefs sustaining the privileges of the whites, including their writers. If the appearance of *Statements after an Arrest* signalled the important inward dimension of Fugard's work, it also demonstrated the difficulties of exploring private tensions and ambivalences at a time of increasingly polarized public debate and activity. But now that the struggle against apartheid has been transformed into something more varied and dispersed – a struggle against poverty, violence and disease, as well as against forgetting – Fugard's more interior dramas beg to be reconsidered and evaluated. By means of their common focus upon inner experience – the dimension of fantasy, dream or nightmare – certain of his plays offer a particularly compelling opportunity to experience and reflect upon the way in which we are all intimately touched by past as well as present tyrannies. They should be thought about in a different way from his more recent memory work, though, the post-1994 plays *The Captain's Tiger* and *Sorrows and Rejoicings*: these, too, emphasize the inner dimension of experience, but in a context free of the pressures to relate to the racially and culturally differentiated 'other' that so marked Fugard's earlier career, and hence free of the overtones of guilt and complicity attaching to his earlier, more inward plays.

The key to these plays, as to so much of his work, is the question of identity, bound up as much with the inheritance of Calvin as with Camus (or Hegel through Camus). How is the self constructed, and what role does conscience play in it? How does it react to the destructive, extreme effects of suffering? What is interesting about them is to see how these questions are articulated theatrically, in terms of staged gestures of a specific, bodily kind. Led by his reading of Grotowski (and radical psychiatrist R. D. Laing's *Politics of Experience* (1967)), as much as by the collaborative play making with the Serpent Players, to rethink the linear, 'mechanical' linkage of his previous work, by 1970 Fugard had embarked on a 'dialogue' with his most important female collaborator, Yvonne Bryceland, to find a new way of 'communicating my sense of self and the world as experienced by that self'. Bryceland shared a struggle to 'discover or feel, if there were not in fact regions of our experience of ourselves that had not been articulated [. . .] We both felt that there were things to say, and ways of saying them, that we had not yet encountered' (*N*. 189–90). The material for exploring these new regions had already been noted, in the early to mid-1960s – for a play about Robben Island, a play about a figure from Camus's *Carnets*, a play about an informer in Algoa Park, Port Elizabeth, and another about a white librarian caught and photographed by the police *in flagrante* with a Coloured Anglican missionary in the small Karoo town of De Aar. The first set of images eventually became *The Island* (1973), the second, *Dimetos* (1975), the third, *A Lesson from Aloes* (1978), and the fourth, *Statements after an Arrest under the Immorality Act* (1972). *Statements* was to prove the most inward and, paradoxically, the most physically extreme and disturbing of these.

Less a play than a choreographed set of variations upon the stark opening image (shocking for its first South African audiences) of a white woman and Coloured man lying in a state of post-coital tenderness on a blanket on the floor, *Statements* transgressed a fundamental assumption of racist ideology: that desire across racial lines was unnatural and should be resisted, if not forcibly stamped out. The law forbidding 'unlawful carnal intercourse' (or indeed 'any immoral or indecent act') between the races alluded to by the title has long been consigned to the dustbin of history; but it existed for nearly three decades (1957–85) as the cornerstone of apartheid interference in private life. The Immorality Act of 1957 was the product of numerous earlier attempts (supported by the Dutch Reformed Churches) to regulate individual behaviour so as to 'preserve' racial distinctiveness; and it brought humiliation, misery and despair to many thousands before it was abolished for having made 'enemies for South Africa'.[3] As Jeanne Colleran has pointed out, while many plays by Fugard (and by other South African dramatists) have presented the effects of apartheid, few have addressed directly this 'very core of the heart of South African racism: the prohibition against skin contact' – a prohibition reflecting a fear so strong, it required the vast bureaucratic machine of the state to prevent, and to punish. Colleran makes a persuasive claim for the continuing validity of the *Statements* play, which, while it exposes the limits of liberal tolerance (in the white librarian's reactions to her lover), reveals also a deep sense of the couple's 'insurmountable dread', swamping 'any occasion for intimacy' and overwhelming 'easy platitudes about reconciliation and forgiveness'. 'However dark', she adds, 'this statement about what had been legally erected but is less easily eradicated, is an extraordinarily vital one, well worth the re-listening.'[4]

Re-watching might be more apt: *Statements* is Fugard's most physically explicit play, taking actors and audiences further from social reality than before, in order to suggest the instinctual dimensions of a tabooed, carnal relationship. Fugard's first reflections upon the original case indicated where he thought he might go: 'The De Aar Immorality Case: outsiders. Violation of a social taboo: incest, homosexuality, adultery. Impossible (absurd), because doomed, love. The essence of love = absurdity. Possession and loss' (N. 187). These large concepts required a new theatrical reality, one that allowed him to explore the ambivalent effects upon the self of all kinds of transgressive desire. The opportunity came after the *Orestes* experiment, when Brian Astbury decided to create a theatre space for Fugard and Bryceland 'to work in', a space where they had 'the right to fail'.[5] Hence the first version of the play was written for the opening of Astbury's Space Theatre in

Cape Town, where it appeared on 28 March 1972, directed by Fugard with himself as the Coloured school principal Errol Philander (whose name could have been more subtly chosen), and Yvonne Bryceland as the shy white librarian Frieda Joubert. Fugard's lovers already live separate existences: she as a spinster alone in the small Karoo town of Noupoort, he with his wife and family outside in the drought-ridden Coloured township, Bontrug. The 'statements' of the title refer both to the charges read out by the arresting officer, and to their final monologues. The intimate, inward emphasis is movingly suggested by the bare, dimly lit opening: a moment of reflection as the man and woman lie on the floor, he caressing her hair while she languorously recounts the events of her day. Already naked, and sated, their situation defeats the potential erotic charge of visible love making or stripping, as the individuality of their bodies (to which they draw attention) resists the commodification or fetishization of them. Yet their relationship, though tender, is fearful: lights (a match) and sounds (a dog barking) disturb them. Their conversation is about books, about the course of their year-long affair, about the differences between town and township.

The differences between their images of themselves soon emerge: the woman's imagination is dominated by images of sterility and isolation; the man's, by the struggle to better himself (he is another aspiring township learner). Beneath their differences, however, there is a pre-cultural, biological level of selfhood, suggested by the woman's memory of seeing two snakes killed while mating, after which the bodies continued to move. The idea of an underlying, instinctual drive that keeps the species going is reinforced by the tissue of allusions to theories of evolution that Fugard added when he revised the play after its first production. The Karoo, with its fossil evidence of early forms of life such as *Australopithicus Africanus*, is, of course, an appropriate setting for such allusions, allusions that coalesce around a repeated phrase, from one of Philander's borrowed books: life evinces 'no vestige of a beginning and no prospect of an end' (*IP* 80). Dividing the lovers is as futile as trying to stop evolution, which is endless.

After the opening sequence, the lovers 'impulsively' unite in an embrace, which remains fixed in a tableau as a plain-clothes policeman comes on to read from a dossier recounting the details of their arrest. In Immorality Act cases photographs were usually taken in evidence, and the next sequence is enacted in a series of nightmarish camera flashes, as the lovers scramble for their clothes, cowering from the light, while babbling disjointed explanations for their 'crime'. Finally, standing in the unremitting glare of two spotlights, they blurt out their 'statements', semi-poetic, fragmentary revelations of how they see themselves after arrest. In pathetic contradiction of the human ordinariness of their relationship, the woman admits guilt, and scrutinizes her body for its faults, while the man thinks of running, before giving up 'all that is left of me', until 'there is nothing left, just my hands, and they are empty' (*IP* 102–5) – a concluding gesture interestingly echoed in the later play about sexual guilt (amongst other things), *Dimetos*.

The sheer physical eloquence of *Statements* focuses a key element of Fugard's drama, shaped to some extent by the dynamics of repulsion and desire in an oppressive society: the struggle to express 'carnal reality'. Five years earlier, while working simultaneously on *Boesman and Lena* and a Serpent Players' piece called *Friday's Bread on Monday*, Fugard had asked himself: 'How can the full reality of a life here and now be stated?' His answer was to re-assert his faith in a representational code he defined as the 'Carnal Reality' of the actor in space and time (*N*. 171). His obsessive concern for the bodily specifics of his chosen performers is apparent in his frequent use of the actor's physical appearance – changing clothes, washing themselves or otherwise drawing attention to their bodies on stage; but it is a concern deepened by the more extreme feelings and situations encountered during the 1970s, when he encouraged performers to mime the actions they were recalling – undressing to display the bare, unaccommodated body (Robert in *Sizwe Bansi*), or urinating on stage (as John does to disinfect Winston's eye-wound in *The Island*). In *Statements* the couple's naked bodies are their only defence, disturbing and challenging the audience by their vulnerability to overcome the voyeurism inherent in their position; although the most challenging moment was yet to come, in *'Master Harold' . . . and the Boys*, when the racial insult at its centre is literalized by the black actor playing Sam presenting his naked backside to his young white 'master' and the audience *'for* [. . .] inspection' *(PEP* 45).

Initial reactions to the *Statements* play in South Africa were confused and contradictory. The drama critic of the Cape *Argus* admired Yvonne Bryceland's 'haunting pathos' and Fugard's own 'grimy realism', in representing a situation 'which has never before been dramatised in so immediate a fashion', nonetheless concluding that 'such things are better at least partly concealed'.[6] The Afrikaans writer Elsa Joubert remarked that *Statements* 'had no political message' despite being 'rooted firmly in the centre of local events'; she felt the audience was turned into an 'unwilling additional player', 'a gruesome experience' that left it uncertain and unfulfilled. The London production a year later, when Ben Kingsley replaced Fugard as Philander, elicited more positive reactions – encapsulated in Robert Cushman's remark that Kingsley's and Bryceland's bodies provided 'the most powerful statement made either before or after their arrest': 'Neither body is glamorous, but both are eloquent, of passion and of shame.'[7]

In a reversal of the order of production in South Africa, the play was preceded by Kani's and Ntshona's stunning performances in *Sizwe Bansi* and *The Island*, which, while guaranteeing full houses, rather overshadowed the sensitive and nuanced acting of Bryceland and Kingsley. Some critics were disconcerted by the play's repetitive structure, its curious hovering between realist and non-realist dimensions – most suggestively in what Fugard called its 'subtextual' moments, when the guilty couple are caught by the flashes of police cameras. But it was in these moments that we realize how part of the lovers' minds supports the logic that condemns them, as John Elsom observed:

> They both regard the temporal justice which snaps them up as some mark of divine retribution. But their bodies do not accept the habits of their minds, which is why, despite the surface bickering, one instinctive movement of the hand or loin destroys the destructive alienation. Physical love, their very nakedness, overcomes the years of conditioning. Throughout the play, Fugard emphasizes those forces, such as evolution and the need for water, which the will of man can't control, only violate. Love is one of those forces, and to separate the lovers is an act of mutilation.[8]

Mutilation, but not death. The man's final monologue as he stands naked before us expresses an alienation more extreme than the woman's, a culmination of all those emasculated men in Fugard – Morris, Johnnie, Boesman – who are robbed of their ability to act, even to function. As in Beckett, it seems as if only words remain.

But the words are abstract, and lack resonance; it is the 'carnal', external images of the two that paradoxically prompt an effective awareness of their trauma. Fugard's people are generally shown living through an awareness of suffering – their own, or that of others; an awareness we may indeed at times find 'gruesome', although that response should lead us to reflect upon ourselves, and our own positions, as passive observers, drawn perhaps unwillingly into a sense of participating in a journey of self-discovery whose outward parameters extend beyond the individual, or historically special case. Of course, pain, guilt, betrayal and a minimal survival are familiar themes in Fugard; so, too, are the moments of tenderness evident briefly between the man and the woman in *Statements* – and between woman and woman in *Dimetos* (and *The Road to Mecca*). But the emphasis upon carnality as a more than merely individual matter is even more important now than when these plays were first produced, as relations between individual subjectivity and place overtake the socio-political discourses of earlier struggles. Intimacy, loyalty and betrayal have become more broadly political issues in southern Africa, as the crises around sexuality (in particular rape and HIV/AIDS) have emerged.

A play like *Statements* forcefully demonstrates that, for Fugard, the disempowered are not definable simply in terms of race. The central characters of many of his plays are white South Africans; of these, a striking number are women, ranging from the middle-aged Milly (in *People Are Living There*), the sad librarian of *Statements* and the frustrated housekeeper Sophia of *Dimetos*, to the psychologically wounded Gladys (in *A Lesson from Aloes*) and the damaged twosome of *The Road to Mecca*. The diversity and depth of character displayed in these works are extraordinary, especially when compared with the more one-dimensional plays of the 'protest' era in South Africa; so, too, is the variety of dramatic resource, including the symbolic or mythical element in

Dimetos, a play that struck many on its first appearance in 1975 as deplorably obscure and (as we have seen) unpolitical. Yet, while it departed from explicitness about the daily experiences of the victims of apartheid to explore instead the inner doubts and self-questioning of a white man among whites in a remote and timeless setting, the play makes once again the claim of the inner life, of interiority – an interiority that implicitly repudiates the boundaries between the political and the non-political, the public and the private.

The opening of *Dimetos* is itself a challenge: to producers, performers and audience. *'Lydia is lowered to the bottom of a well to tie ropes around a horse that has fallen down'* (IP 111) must rank as one of the more extraordinary stage directions in modern theatre. For the early productions, Fugard directed that this should be managed on a stage empty apart from a bench and a rope – which the engineer Dimetos has then to throw down to the half-naked young woman standing a few feet away in dim light, where she pretends she is astride a desperate horse down a well. Lydia has to carry out instructions bellowed down to her by her uncle, by tying a sling around the horse to bring it back to the surface. One ingenious solution (at the 1981 production at The People's Space in Cape Town) was to isolate the man and the girl in single spots, the latter crouching within a gauze tube suspended from the rafters to suggest a well, while a rope was worked through an overhead pulley connecting them in their joint struggle to free the beast. The sensuality of the opening image is important, as is the sense of struggle, and the need for both give and take implicit in the pulley's action. The horse is a traditional image of sensual power, reinforced by the girl twisting about as she straddles its heaving body, anticipating a major theme of the play – the vain struggle to control desire, a carnal force now imagined as powerful as gravity, although that would mean it is beyond the realm of human responsibility, too.

Responsibility requires a confrontation with the inner self, before there can develop a sense of the other. The self-exiled engineer Dimetos is shown failing to manage this, with pathetic if not tragic results – a predicament the playwright originally found in this enigmatic paragraph from Camus's *Carnets*, dated August 1939:

70

Dimetos had a guilty love for his niece, who hanged herself. One day, the little waves carried onto the fine sand of the beach the body of a marvelously beautiful young woman. Seeing her, Dimetos fell on his knees, stricken with love. But he was forced to watch the decay of this magnificent body, and went mad. This was his niece's vengeance, and the symbol of a condition we must try to define.[9]

Desire, betrayal, guilt and vengeance are the key elements in this mythical kernel (apparently derived from a little-known first century BC Greek poet, Parthenius).[10] As he 're-read and thought about it many times', this situation 'commanded' Fugard's imagination until finally, despite being 'very far away, both in time and distance, from my own social realities', the moment came to keep the 'appointment I had made with myself' to represent it.[11]

Camus found the Dimetos story apt on the eve of war in Europe; for Fugard, Dimetos seems to echo the playwright's own thoughts at the time, when he tells the young man who comes to claim him for the troubled city that he is 'tired of other men's needs, other men's disasters' (IP 136). But the inactive engineer goes on to use the unwitting emissary Danilo to arrange a sexual assault on his orphaned niece, which he watches from an adjoining lemon grove – an action that invites us to watch with him, making us voyeurs in our turn. The telltale lemon smell on Dimetos's hands reveals his complicity in what happens, which leads the girl to hang herself, using knots her uncle had taught her – retribution, too, seems as strong as gravity. This concludes the first act. The second act, some years later, finds Dimetos and Sophia (who secretly loves him) beside the sea, where the smell from a rotting offshore creature drives him mad. After Sophia has revealed her own sense of responsibility in the niece's suicide, she delivers a nightmare vision that was Yvonne Bryceland's gift to the playwright – a monologue prompted by Fugard's request to her to go and look at Blake's *Hecate* in the Tate Gallery in London, an image of the triformed moon goddess and guardian of the underworld derived from *Macbeth*'s Queen of the Witches.[12] Sophia recalls going on a long walk, to find a woman immobile beside a 'dark and turgid pool', as day turns to night.

71

SOPHIA. [. . .] That is where I found her . . . sitting, waiting for me . . . her knees drawn up under her chin. Her feet are misshapen . . . her hair, long and soft, lies gently around her face. But it's all a lie. There is something wrong with her. She keeps company with a donkey, an owl, a griffin, a bat, and an old, million-year-old turtle.

There is a terrible familiarity between herself and the entrance to hell, which is just behind her. She goes in and out. She was waiting for me. If I could tell you . . . If you could help me . . . I loved Dimetos.

(*IP* 161)

Blake's prophetic writings, which appeal for a reconciliation of self and other, provide an intertext for this play, with its resounding Blakean epigraph, 'May God us keep/From Single vision & Newton's sleep'. Sophia's vision is as narrow in its way as Dimetos' Newtonian dreams of control through knowledge, and she cannot help him with the love she confesses, hence her departure. But why is she associated with the grotesquerie of hell? Presumably because she represents the evil aspect of the female principle, while Lydia represented the good.

Interestingly prophetic of the suicidal figure of Miss Helen in *The Road to Mecca* (also first played with extraordinary conviction by Bryceland), Sophia remains a somewhat undeveloped character, leaving Dimetos alone with his self-lacerating guilt, when she might have engaged with him. Like her, he is trapped in the solipsistic self. Towards the end, he is left scrabbling for shells, reminiscent of some early southern African *strandloper* or prehistoric nomad, the first human on these shores. His position is both an escape from history, and an attempt to anticipate it. 'What must I do?' (*IP* 162), he asks. The ending of the play provides the answer, as his dead niece's spectral, offstage voice miraculously offers the chance to redeem himself: by confessing his guilt, and the inadequacy of his kind of knowledge, and by relearning how to create – which he does by turning it all into a story, beginning again with what happened at the beginning of the play, with the age-old narrative opening 'Once upon a time . . .', as his hands imitate a juggler who could 'give and take with the same action' (*IP* 163–4). The play thereby concludes by calling for the 'long-term' investment in an interactive skill basic to its creator Fugard's aesthetic, and, ironically, drawn from the social context so markedly absent from it – the context of black storytellers whose oral traditions have underpinned South African cultural expression from time immemorial, and that Fugard used so effectively in his township work.

If his broken engineer may be redeemed, it is through forgiveness for the sinful exercise of power; but the hands he holds out to us at the end (like Prospero at the end of *The Tempest*, particularly as played by Paul Scofield shortly before he was cast as Dimetos) – these hands remain tainted, it seems to me, because of his isolation and wilful ignorance. A 'gesture of humanist complicity', one critic called it,[13] although, if we attribute an Afrikaner identity to the character (as played by Carel Trichardt in the Edinburgh original, and then by Marius Weyers in the People's Space version), his attitude can be understood to reflect a certain brooding Calvinism, of suffering without grace, that troubles Fugard as it troubled many of his compatriots. Confirmation of this reading may be found in the play's companion piece, the film drama *The Guest at Steen-kampskraal* (1977), in which he himself went on to perform another guilt-obsessed Afrikaner, the poet-naturalist Eugène Marais. As John Elsom, almost alone among critics at the time, understood, *Dimetos* is in some senses

> not Fugard's least, but perhaps his most, 'South African' play. He has journeyed, not away from his home, but deeper into the heart of it. The mythological framework is not an escape from 'reality' but a sort of shield to protect himself and others from the painful glare of self-examination [. . . it] is a stern, demanding play, an authentic tragedy seen from the angle of an Afrikaner, which makes no concessions to Western liberalism. Apartheid is not mentioned, although it would be the obvious illustration for the attempt to crush nature.[14]

The central conflict between guilty withdrawal and taking responsibility was more convincingly demonstrated by casting as Dimetos Afrikaans performers, like Marius Weyers, whose 'strongly controlled playing', building from the 'relatively placid, withdrawn, ostensibly avuncular figure' of the opening, to 'the ultimately raging, demented guilt-ridden soul whose scientific knowledge cannot rescue him from his moral dilemma' at the end, helped focus the meaning of the work.[15]

Yet the landscape of *Dimetos* is ultimately the shifting, uncertain inner landscape of guilt and responsibility, represented in resonantly mythological terms (Prometheus and Faust also hover behind Dimetos); and, as such, it is part of Fugard's struggle to represent the unrepresentable, to make the unconscious, conscious. Far from denying the public sphere, the play draws us into acknowledging its inseparability from the private life, in a society seeking irrevocably to demarcate the two. If, as Michael Rustin has argued, the difficult but necessary task today is to connect the representation of the interior, perhaps unconscious experiences of individuals with their wider social determinations and representations,[16] then *Dimetos* helps point the way. So, too, did *The Guest at Steenkampskraal*: first shown with this full title on BBC TV in March 1977, and, like *Dimetos*, largely ignored since, *The Guest* (as it has been subsequently known) has suffered from being interpreted in rather limited, realist terms; viewed as a more symbolic, even gothic-expressionist piece (like something by the recent Afrikaans dramatist Reza De Wet), it takes its place beside *Dimetos* as another attempt on Fugard's part to explore the nature of suffering and the inevitability of guilt.

While both works deal with the self-examination of isolated artist-figures, *The Guest* was more specific and detailed: set on a farm in the remote Heidelberg district of the Transvaal in 1926, with Marais depicted as a writer struggling to understand himself in relation to his people and his environment, animal and natural, the film suggested a man whose reflections on the problem of suffering and redemption drive him mad. Quoting directly from Marais, Fugard reflects upon how silence falls upon a troop of chacma baboons at sunset, the older members assuming

> attitudes of profound dejection. It is hardly possible to avoid the conclusion that the chacma suffers from the same attribute of pain which is such an important ingredient of human mentality, and that the condition is due to the same cause, namely, the suffering inseparable from the new mind which like man the chacma has acquired in the course of its evolution. (*IP* 204)

74

Marais's dark vision is represented in the form of dreamlike images accompanied by voiceover quotations like this from *The Soul of the Ape* (published posthumously in 1969); in his drug-induced madness, he echoes *Othello* – 'I can thy former light restore if I repent me' (*IP* 214) – seeking like Dimetos a saving grace, but with self-destructive consequences, as his addiction returns. Fugard dealt with this – an analogy for his alcoholism – again in his 'personal parable', *A Place with the Pigs* (1987), as a struggle for freedom from internalized constraint.

Turning inward for Fugard has meant expressing a more pessimistic view of life. Not (*pace* Elsom) tragic: none of his figures has the necessary greatness to generate tragedy, and Dimetos is ultimately a small man, persuaded by the blind love of those closest to him, as well as the adulation of the more distant, that his plight is universal, when it is his own and self-created. He is, after all, a white South African, not a mythical Greek; indeed, as I have been suggesting, an Afrikaner, indulging in escapist fantasies about a pre-industrial, feudal and patriarchal social order that might guarantee the harmony and security absent from the present. Fugard reveals a yearning for this ideal, while recognizing that it is a kind of psychosis, too, the product of guilt. His understanding of these matters can easily be underestimated, through overdeterministic contextual readings, although of course it is hard to ignore the fact that production of works like *Statements* or *Dimetos* or *The Guest* during the 1970s coincided with the collapse of liberal politics in the country, and the rise of the Black Consciousness Movement, when thousands of young black South Africans were fleeing abroad, many to train for the forthcoming conflict. White opposition from within had become futile and irrelevant, international opposition was 'though strong in rhetoric, weak in substance'.[17]

So these plays emerge, not just from an embattled society, but from an embattled segment within that society: a segment characterizable as that of 'the colonizer who refuses'; those whose dissent, though principled, appears to have had little influence beyond arousing the anger of fellow citizens, while leaving the colonized indifferent.[18] Fugard was perceived by the authorities as a danger; and by a minority of theatre-

75

workers, critics and audiences as a significant voice. But how far dissenting, liberal or left-wing artists and intellectuals such as him unconsciously share the assumptions of the dominant power structure they consciously reject remains a question. It is a question raised by all his plays, with varying degrees of self-awareness; his more inward works depict one way of addressing it.

What has rarely been acknowledged is the religious or visionary tendency of this work, another aspect of his witnessing: focusing upon the suffering body, the actor's carnal reality, carries with it the ready implication of a need to move beyond sociocultural or material determination. Fugard himself has never denied this potential in his plays, and there can be little doubt of the religious, at times specifically Christian aspect of *Dimetos*, *The Road to Mecca*, *A Place with the Pigs* and even *Playland*, all of which involve a quasi-mythical dynamic of penance, forgiveness and redemption, although all of them, too, carefully avoid overtly religious characters, with the striking exception of the small town 'dominee' or minister Marius Byleveld, in *The Road to Mecca*, whose Dutch Reformed faith is treated with respect, despite its manifest inadequacy when confronted by the personal artistic vision of the elderly Miss Helen. But this inadequacy is perhaps the point: Fugard's plays do not exclude the appeal of the transcendent; rather, they imply it is a function of individual choice in the face of human suffering and travail, guaranteeing nothing. *Boesman and Lena* may be said to express a Manichaean vision of darkness, only alleviated momentarily by Lena's dance; *The Road to Mecca*, as its title implies, explores the possibility of light.

By the time *The Road to Mecca* premiered at Yale in 1984 it had become clear that a new phase of play making had arrived, with Fugard returning to a more conventional form of production, abandoning the improvisational and collaborative techniques he had been using with the Serpent Players and Yvonne Bryceland, and the extremism of *Statements* and *Dimetos*. Like *A Lesson from Aloes*, *The Road to Mecca* is set in an earlier period, avoiding any direct engagement with the difficulties of the present that, with the declaration of a State of Emergency in 1984, were reaching a crisis. Instead, Fugard chose to continue the trend set by *Dimetos*, *The Guest*, and, to a lesser extent, *'Master Harold'* . . . *and the Boys*: of exploring the psychology of the isolated white consciousness, and in particular, the nature of the artist and the artist's concerns.

The central character of *The Road to Mecca*, Miss Helen Martins, is based on a Nieu Bethesda eccentric who committed suicide in 1976, some two years after Fugard had begun visiting the remote village on a regular basis. The play takes place in the glass-encrusted living room of the eccentric Miss Helen (as she is called in the play), whose bizarre sculptures and refusal to attend church have caused outrage in the 'almost feudal' Afrikaner community ('A Note on Miss Helen', *RM*). Shunned by those around her, she faces a dilemma, dramatized by her two visitors: Byleveld, the upright local minister who wants her to retire to a Sunshine Home for the Aged, and Elsa, a young liberal schoolteacher from Cape Town who also believes her friend cannot cope. The minister's pastoral concern masks possessive desires, while the schoolteacher's surface liberalism has been tested and found wanting by an encounter with a black woman named Patience, walking the Karoo roads with her baby on her back after being evicted from a farm. The two-act play explores the potential for resistance of the frail older woman towards the two opposing forces she faces, and concludes with a vibrant image of the increasingly dark and gloomy stage suddenly turned incandescent as she orders Elsa to light the candles to celebrate her independence, as well as her artistic vision: of 'Mecca' as a 'city of light and colour more splendid than anything I had ever imagined' (*RM* 72).

The resolution of past trauma for Elsa (who has had an abortion) and Miss Helen (many years a lonely and depressed widow), however, obscures the question left at the end: what about the 'good old South African story' (*RM* 20) of the destitute black woman on the road, whose presence – based on a personal encounter – prompted Fugard initially to name the play after her? As Elsa exclaims towards the end: 'She won't leave me alone, Helen. [. . .] There's no Mecca waiting for her at the end of the road' (*RM* 76). Indeed not. The meeting between anguished white liberal and stoic victim, which is referred to three times in the play, raises a demand that is not

77

met by Fugard's focus upon Miss Helen's struggle for personal freedom against patriarchy and an uncomprehending community, a struggle for the aesthetic of 'pagan' carnality expressed in her curiously Blakean sculptures. Transcendence cannot be bought quite so easily. Nevertheless, the last gesture of the play, as Miss Helen blows out the candles she has lit to show her visitor – and the audience – her glass-encrusted, visionary house, then watches wistfully as the smoke rises slowly into the gathering darkness, suggests an artist aware of an inability to control more than a private, interior world. Courageously, however, Fugard will continue to try and do so.

5

Memory Plays

The central concern of Fugard's more recent writing has been the importance of his personal past. This includes embarking upon a projected four-part prose memoir – the first part of which, *Cousins*, appeared in 1994, that *annus mirabilis* for South Africa. The playwright has been redefining himself, now that his familiar role as his country's witness has apparently been overtaken. This has meant redefining his role in relation to his and his country's past, and in particular how he has become who he is – a 'bastardized Afrikaner'. This chapter traces the significance of memory and the past in his recent work, while dipping back to the play that first opened this particular floodgate in 1982 – *'Master Harold'* . . . *and the Boys*. As plays such as *Valley Song* (1995), *The Captains's Tiger* (1997) and *Sorrows and Rejoicings* (2001) suggest, the task of memory in South Africa (and indeed in the post-colonial world more generally) is not about reconstructing a whole past, supposing that were possible; it is about recreating images of the past that recollect pain and suffering, while allowing for recovery. Such images are at the centre of these Fugard plays. The difficulty of interpreting them, however, is well suggested by a comparison recorded by Walter Benjamin, who was interested in the analogy between memory and photographic images: the past, he said, deposited images in literary texts like those 'caught on a light-sensitive plate. Only the future has at its disposal a developer strong enough to let the image appear in all its details.'[1]

Benjamin's analogy is doubly apposite. Fugard's theatre has always been interested in historically charged imagery, sometimes even taking photographs as their origin, as in *Sizwe Bansi Is Dead*, or using photography as a means of subtextual suggestiveness, as in *Statements after an Arrest under the Immorality Act* – an interest even more evident in his recent memory work: the opening chapter of *Cousins* (which is fully illustrated with photographs) analyses a 'Family Photo', and *The Captain's Tiger* features a photograph of his mother coming to life dramatically. Yet if, as Benjamin suggests, we cannot determine what the future may read in these images, perhaps we can begin to sense some of their implications, as the years pass and we become the future.

Fugard's new awareness of the ways in which his personal past, through memory, may be recovered and explored as a response to the present is not unique, as recent South African poetry (by, for example, Karen Press) has demonstrated; nor are South Africans alone in acknowledging the importance of recalling the traumas of the past, as the continuing interest of, for example, Holocaust memories for writers, historians, literary critics and theorists demonstrates. But the need for people who have experienced the more extreme impact of apartheid – the abuse, torture and murders of the dying years of that desperate system – to see and hear about, indeed to witness, what happened during the apartheid years continues. In the context of the Truth and Reconciliation Commission (TRC), which began hearings in 1996 and published its report in 1998, or the new Apartheid Museum (2001), plays about memory, even when they seem to have relatively little explicit connection with their times, have a peculiar significance and value. And even a small-scale, 'sublime memory play'[2] like *'Master Harold' . . . and the Boys* resonates in terms of a broader politics of both personal and public, both inner and outer spheres of life – in so far as these are finally separable.

Fugard has never shown much interest in the historical past, unlike Brecht, whose influence upon him was always more dramaturgical than ideological; instead, when his plays consciously or unconsciously reach back in time, it is usually to those earlier periods of his own life, when the ground was being laid for his 'appointments', the most striking example of which is *'Master Harold'*. This work has been considered by many, especially in the USA, to be his masterpiece – a view that reflects the extraordinary receptiveness to it abroad. At a Sunday matinée performance that Albert Wertheim attended in New York, for example, the audience became unusually still, and then 'groaned and wept' at the events on stage, until finally bursting out into 'thunderous' applause, 'so moved by what they had witnessed, so aware of its relevance to their own American lives, that they filed out in uncommon silence'.[3] But it was not only American audiences that were thus moved: as I can testify, the reaction to the Market Theatre production at the National Theatre's Cottesloe Theatre in London in 1983 was, if not quite so unreservedly emotional, both tearful and enthusiastic. The local South African reaction was more muted, but, as Joseph Lelyveld saw in Johannesburg, the 'multiracial audience' at the Market premiere was 'visibly shaken', those who did not join in the standing ovation at the end 'seemingly plunged' into 'a private world of grief and loss'.[4] Responses to a local revival (at the Baxter, Cape Town, 1999) suggest continuing audience upset.

Such strong emotions are generated by a play that runs without interval the realistic hundred minutes of its action, building to a climax as shocking as it is unexpected, when the teenage white boy at its centre spits in the face of one of his mother's black servants, who up to then has replaced his absent father in affection and loyalty. It is one of the modern theatre's most disturbing moments; and it is perhaps no surprise to know that, while based on an incident in Fugard's past that it took him his whole career up to then to disclose, it aroused in audiences everywhere feelings of shock and disbelief, followed by guilt (among whites) and anger (among blacks) – and, one can but hope, a greater awareness and understanding of the secret roots of racist violence.

The play is strongly autobiographical. As an adolescent, Fugard, like the character Hally who is modelled on him and whose name was once his own, developed a close friendship with one of his mother's black waiters at the Jubilee Residential Hotel, a man named Sam Semela (Sam in the play), who was with the family for fifteen years, and who went on to work for them at the St George's Park Tearoom. Despite the gap in race, age and education, the man and the boy became so close that Fugard has referred to Semela as 'the most significant – the only – friend of my boyhood years'. While Fugard shared his precocious juvenile reading with Semela, and Sam shared

81

his experience and wisdom with Hally, the gap between them seemed to disappear. But one day there was a 'rare quarrel' between them, the subject of which is forgotten. Silently they closed the tearoom, and made for home, Sam on foot to New Brighton, Hally following on his bicycle. As he passed Sam, he called out his name and, 'out of a spasm of acute loneliness', spat in his face. Recalling the event years later, Fugard did not suppose he would 'ever deal with the shame' that overwhelmed him 'the second after I had done that' (N. 25–6).

But he did eventually try and deal with that shame: after turning over in his mind for some time in the early 1980s the idea for a play centring on an image of two black servants, the crystallizing realization came that they should be seen in relationship to a white boy – himself.[5] He had, he said, arrived at that moment that 'totally symbolised the ugliness, the potential ugliness waiting for me as a white South African', an experience of his own as well as his country's racism. 'The play is an attempt to share that experience with the audience.'[6] Clearly he succeeded: the exorcism of his private guilt provided the opportunity for an exorcism of public guilt. This is more than merely a matter of white liberal breast beating, despite liberal enthusiasm for the play at home and abroad. We are invited to identify with Hally's rejection of his friend and father-figure, but not only is this rejection shown to be the outcome of rage and humiliation, it is at the cost of turning away those whose labour and affection will subsequently be redirected towards each other, a move that suggests the future and black empowerment.

In that sense, the image at the end of the play, when the 'master' becomes an isolated boy, and the 'boys' two mature men in harmony with each other, offers one answer to Fugard's quest for the power of imagination he sought while completing Boesman and Lena, to anticipate the future. On one level, the play may be construed as a call for the radical change then about to take place in the country, although, of course, on the personal level, it is, as Errol Durbach has well put it, 'an act of atonement and moral reparation', to the memory of the two men, Sam Semela and 'H.D.F.' – 'the Black and White fathers to whom it is dedicated'.[7] Harold David Fugard died after a long illness in 1961; Sam Semela died in 1983, shortly before John Kani (who acted Sam in South Africa) arrived in New Brighton to take him to see the play. Fugard first thought of subtitling it 'A Personal Memoir', and certainly the setting is unusually detailed and realistic, including the use of music to date as well as punctuate the action. It is structurally simple, as befits such a concentrated, didactic work (Wertheim calls it a *Lehrstück*). It opens like a photo coming to life: we take in the 1950s tearoom appurtenances, including a serving counter on one side and a jukebox on the other, with a small table and chair downstage, a chalkboard and telephone, before the two black men appear: Willie, sleeves and trousers rolled up, kneeling carefully on a folded piece of cardboard as he mops the floor; Sam, wearing the brass-buttoned white jacket, white shirt, black bow tie and trousers of a waiter, leaning nonchalantly on the table, as he pages idly through a comic book. Willie gets up and swings heavily into a dance step with an imaginary partner, which leads into a discussion of the forthcoming New Brighton Ballroom Competition. Sam instructs him how to avoid mistakes. Like Robert/Sizwe and Styles before them, the two offer a physical contrast: Willie as awkward as Sam is graceful, Sam imagining an ideal world of happy dancers, Willie thinking of the harsh reality of his frightened partner, Hilda – the black woman who, invisible in this play (as Patience is invisible in *Mecca*), reminds us of Lena, and the dreadful hierarchy of power under racial oppression.

As in all Fugard's best work, the play's central theme, of isolation, community and the existential need to choose between them, rises apparently inevitably out of the relationship established between the three characters. The terrible loneliness brought about by the betrayal at its centre will be offset by the idea of dancing as a paradigm of harmony. But harmony seems as out of reach for whites as the kite that Sam once made for Hally – whose arrival interrupts the opening conversation between the two men, and who departs at the end, leaving them together again. 'Master Harold', as Willie respectfully addresses him, tells the men about his schoolwork, and, uninterrupted by customers as the rain patters continuously down outside, the three spend the rest of the afternoon following the threads of shared memory, alternately bantering and serious, that this uncovers – jarred only by telephone calls from the hospital, where Hally's father is being treated for his amputated leg. These calls provoke the frustrated, unhappy outbursts that culminate in Hally's abuse of Sam, his surrogate father. He brusquely orders the men to 'Get on with it!' after the first call (*PEP* 27). Sam's attempt to console the boy by invoking the pleasure of dancing, 'like being in a dream about a world where accidents don't happen' (*PEP* 36), is destroyed by the second phone call: his father is, after all, coming home. 'So much for a bloody world without collisions,' cries Hally. 'Do you want to know what is really wrong with your lovely little dream, Sam? [. . .] You left out the cripples' (*PEP* 41). Reckless with despair, he conjures up an image reminiscent of the end of *Hello and Goodbye*: 'a bloody comical sight. I mean, it's bad enough on two legs . . . but one and a pair of crutches!' (*PEP* 41). 'It's a terrible sin for a son to mock his father with jokes like that,' urges Sam; but, when Hally then repeats a racialist pun told him by his father, about black 'arses' not being 'fair', Sam tears off his jacket, lowers his trousers, and '*presents his backside for Hally's inspection*'. The boy cannot look. Then, when Sam puts a forgiving hand on his shoulder, he turns and spits in the man's face, expressing the contempt he is unable to show his father (*PEP* 41–5).

As in the climactic moment of *The Blood Knot/Blood Knot*, violence seems imminent, and the tension at this point in the theatre is almost unbearable. With awful self-control, Sam wipes his face, and suggests they 'try again', reminding the boy of the time he carried Hally's drunken father home on his back, the boy following with the crutches; and of when they flew the kite, and Hally thought Sam could join him on a bench marked 'Whites Only': 'You know what that bench means now, and you can leave it any time you choose. All you've got to do is stand up and walk away from it' (*PEP* 48). What the play has made us realize is how difficult that 'all' is; further, how incapable Hally is of accepting reconciliation, as he stumbles off into the dark, leaving the two men dancing slowly together to the strains of Sarah Vaughan's *Little Man You're Crying* on the jukebox – a resonant image of brotherhood, from which the white 'master' has excluded himself.

Emphasizing forgiveness rather than retaliation at the climactic moment led to criticism at the time, although post-1990 this emphasis makes '*Master Harold*' seem more rather than less relevant. Zakes Mokae, long settled in the USA, and whom Fugard cast as Sam for the premiere there, reported one black audience member calling out to him to 'kick Hally's ass'. 'But', Mokae pointed out, for him Fugard's play belonged to a 'different era', and 'you have to understand the difference in Sam's background' as well: an 'illegal' from Lesotho, who would get sent back to his rural home if he was not careful.[8] That is one way of seeing it. But, in any case, Fugard always defuses violence, while showing why it is likely in the given situation. And the idea of art promulgated in the play is of using the imagination to try and construct images of wholeness and harmony out of the corrosive impact of everyday suffering – past and present. Significantly, as the two black men teach the white boy, such images include precisely those popular township cultural activities Hally's English master would consider 'primitive', like the 1950 New Brighton Ballroom Dancing finals for which Sam and Willie are practising (*PEP* 34–5). Fugard's legitimation of township culture through his collaborative work with the Sophiatown and New Brighton performers here finds its poignant farewell coda.

Yet, as I am suggesting, '*Master Harold*' also looks ahead. To a degree well beyond such other plays of the 1970s and 1980s as *Dimetos*, *The Road to Mecca* or *A Place with the Pigs*, '*Master Harold*' connects with the present, if not the future as well, through its concern with the psychology of racism rather than apartheid's legal structures, and by its anticipation of the emergence of black consciousness. By exploring the complex pleasures and pains of an interracial relationship before apartheid really began to bite, '*Master Harold*' reaches across to the time when that legislation has disappeared, but not the social and psychological impulses that made it possible in the first place. Ironically, however, it was the play's physical and verbal explicitness rather than any implication of empowerment for which it was initially banned in South Africa.

Fugard's first memory play was both popular and important; when he turned towards contemporary events, and the new traumas of transformation, simultaneously premiering his plays back in South Africa again, the result was disappointing. In two plays that appeared on the cusp of change, *My Children!*

My Africa! and *Playland*, he bravely tried to salvage a new role for the liberal viewpoint in an increasingly turbulent present. Set in a Karoo schoolroom in 1984, *My Children! My Africa!* is a three-hander that places a young black township activist, Thami, in opposition to his elderly teacher, 'Mr M', who gets 'necklaced' for collaborating with the white authorities, while the white schoolgirl Isabel is left to pronounce his epitaph: 'The future is still ours, Mr M' (*MM* 68). The ambiguities of this somewhat forced conclusion suggest an inability to handle the immediate realities of the time.[9] Similarly problematic, the ironically titled *Playland* was set in a travelling amusement park on the outskirts of a Karoo town on New Year's Eve 1989, where two men, a young white returnee from the border war (Gideon) and a middle-aged black nightwatchman (Martinus), meet and provoke each other into shared revelations about their past crimes. Fugard's 'catalyst' was a photographed atrocity, but the demand for mutual forgiveness and reconciliation that underpins the play's development, as it underpinned the negotiations then underway in the country, was diffused by the moral imbalance between Gideon's involvement in that atrocity with Martinus's murder of his wife's white rapist.

On the other hand, Fugard's main point seems deeply felt: that violence breeds further violence unless there comes a moment in which trying to balance rights and wrongs is set aside for reconciliation; and in that sense *Playland* was timely: some even saw it as a 'healing play'.[10] It suggests another aspect of the impulse to bear witness to his time and place: in terms of memory as a phenomenon to be articulated theatrically. This impulse finds more impressive embodiment in his first so-called post-apartheid play, *Valley Song* (1995) – the first play in which, as he put it, the 'stark, energizing polarity' of the apartheid years, 'when it was so easy to identify the enemy', had gone, and with it his sense of the need 'to speak for a silenced majority'.[11] *Valley Song* was preceded by one last attempt to use workshop techniques to create a theatrical space for other voices – *My Life*, premiered at the National Arts Festival three months after the April 1994 elections. An orchestration of the images and stories of five young women from a range of class and racial or ethnic identities, *My Life* revealed Fugard mediating and shaping the 'new South Africa' in terms of memories and reflections from which he for once excluded himself. The five young performers narrate their own widely different lives, before turning finally to the audience to ask what they think. Although a slight work, its transgressive energies suggested the potential of local theatre at a time when it seemed to be lost in nostalgia or uncertainty – with the exception of emerging feminist and gay theatrework by writer-performers such as Fatima Dike, Sue-Pam Grant, Peter Hayes and Jay Pather.

But, if *My Life* directed attention away from Fugard's desire to tell his own story, defusing to some extent the patriarchal presumption lurking behind the use of female voices elsewhere in his work, in his next play he surprised everyone by putting himself on stage as a neo-Brechtian narrator who directly addresses the audience at both beginning and end, opening himself to criticism as the self-styled Author who interferes in his own stories. *Valley Song* flicks between past and present to suggest a link with the massive changes then taking place in the country, while raising a number of challenging questions by means of this authorial presence; yet it is far from engaging directly with contemporary events, such as the trial in 1995–6 of Eugène 'Prime Evil' de Kock, head of the counter-insurgency unit at Vlakplaas near Pretoria, which was exposing unimaginable depths of depravity among those trying to stop change, while extending the chain of responsibility to top levels of government. Setting a play in the rural backwater of a Karoo village enabled Fugard to avoid these realities, while continuing to propose that, in the long term, individual choice and a respect for the other were what mattered. It was left to playmakers such as the brilliant Handspring Puppet Company to find ways of dealing with the grotesque and appalling revelations of the time, as they did in *Faustus in Africa* (1995) and *Ubu and the Truth Commission* (1997).

But, unlike such ambitious, multi-authored and multimedia productions, Fugard's preferred arena remains the modest, small-scale, bare and intimate theatre of *Valley Song*: a two-hander, with three characters – a 17-year-old Coloured girl, Veronica, who lives with her churchgoing 76-year-old grandfather Abraam or 'Buks' Jonkers, and the Author – an incoming white man, who tells us about and listens to the other two, as we listen to him. The same actor plays both 'Buks' and the Author – Fugard himself in the first performances, in Johannesburg, New York and London. The time is the present, the setting the village of *The Road to Mecca* – Nieu Bethesda. On one level, the play is simply about desire, the desire of the young woman to leave for the big city; and the desire of her grandfather to prevent her departure, to keep the status quo. The white man's desire is for the land, which Buks has worked all his life as a tenant farmer. The play raises the question of who really owns that land. In South Africa, as in other settler-colonial territories in the process of decolonization, such as (most notably) Zimbabwe, the basic demand of the historically dispossessed for the return of the land has to be met, although that is not proving easy. Nor is it in the play.

Valley Song also raises questions about the role and function of theatre. The meta-theatrical role of the character called Author, subsequently performed by Fugard's favourite Afrikaans actor Marius Weyers, is clear from the opening, when the Author stands and speaks directly to the audience about 'his' village in the Karoo, where the 'genuine' white pumpkin seeds grow (the vegetable metaphor is pursued throughout). He then asks us to imagine the character Buks, whose role he takes on (a subtle shift, signalled by putting on a hat and making his body a little more bent) as he murmurs the fragmentary memory of a song Buks heard with the Cape Corps during the war: 'Lae donder mobili'. The unwitting recollection of Verdi's *Rigoletto* introduces the central theme of song as an expression of memory and desire, subtly reinforced in production by musical (guitar) accompaniment.

Fugard's role in *Valley Song*, as writer, director, actor and two characters of different racial origins, hints at the patriarchal aspect of his theatrical activities over the years; it also suggests a connection between his changing personal sense of identity and the nation's developing sense of itself as increasingly aware of its mixed origins. Playing both white settler and Coloured victim as a matter of no more than subtle shifts of gesture – a woolly hat, a change of accent and a stoop identifies Buks – allows Fugard to testify to his faith in the closeness, indeed the identity, of the men in cultural if not racial terms. The extensive use of untranslated Afrikaans in the play (including the Author/Buks and Veronica singing together the hymn 'Die Heiland is Gebore' (The Saviour is Born)), asserts a new sense of that language as one belonging to both black and white voices – historically accurate, but long denied by apartheid-mongers. Yet the main thrust of the play – in which the naive young singer has to face both her grandfather's anxieties about her imminent departure, and the cynicism of the white man who tests her ambitions – prompts the question of how far Fugard still reflects local realities, especially now that he has effectively removed himself from the country about which he nonetheless continues to write. Veronica provides one answer, anticipating Rebecca in *Sorrows and Rejoicings*: the daughter of generations of servants, her naive desires may be threatened by the triumphalism of the first years of the new dispensation, but they remain important, expressing the driving needs of those who remain marginalized.

The setting of *Valley Song* recalls the Karoo pastoral of earlier South African literary tradition, but it is a pastoral coming into collision with modernity. Buks and Veronica are more than merely two 'arme ou kleurlinge' (poor old Coloureds) – a derogatory Afrikaans phrase rejected by Veronica even as she uses it because, as she says, things have changed for them (*VS* 28). Have they changed enough? Buks dreads losing his patch of lovingly tended earth to the incoming white man (based on Fugard's own arrival in the village), and yet the old man is unwilling to ask for his new rights from the country's first democratic government.

> BUKS. You think those groot Kokkedoore [cock-a-doodle-dos] are going to worry about me and my few akkers [acres]? Anyway, I don't think they even know where the village is. You told me yourself once that you couldn't even find us on the map.
> VERONICA. That was the school map, Oupa! Don't be silly now. The Government doesn't sit down with a school map and try to find all the places where it must do things. It already knows where everybody is. We had the elections here, didn't we? . . . just like all the other places in the country.
>
> (*VS* 26)

The humour does not obscure the fact that Buks, who has already lost both wife and daughter to the desire for change, is terrified of it, and clings to Veronica; or the fact that her need for fulfilment will lead her to challenge his authority, even at the cost of his love, so that, when he tries to ignore her pleas for escape, she forces him to listen to her.

This is a turning point in the play, simultaneously focusing attention upon Fugard's move from speaking on behalf of the silenced others, towards offering a space for others to speak. Veronica does not speak for herself, in the sense that, for example, writer-performer Gcina Mhlophe's Zandile speaks for her creator's personal experiences in *Have You Seen Zandile?* (1986), an autobiographical play that also explored in intense and moving detail the quest for independence of a young black woman from the rural areas. Nor is Veronica denied agency – at least in so far as the Author-figure and her grandfather are obliged to listen, when she refuses the demeaning role of housemaid occupied by her mother and grandmother before her, and wishes instead her dream of becoming a famous singer. The audience knows it is only a dream; not only because of what we are told about the fate of those who leave for the bright lights of the city, but also because of the transparent simplicity of her songs, such as 'Railway Bus O Railway Bus', which upsets her grandfather because it brings back memories of when her mother left, and all the other things he would prefer to forget, such as her mother's death in Johannesburg (*VS* 12–14).

Memory and forgetting are central to *Valley Song*, as they are to any society struggling to change. So, too, are nostalgia and an unwillingness to face the future. The Author admits at the end of the play that the future belongs to Veronica, while wishing that the Valley could 'stay the unspoilt, innocent little world it was when I first discovered it [. . .] I am not as brave about change as I would like to be', he confesses, before she finally departs (*VS* 53). That is as much as she can do; her power lies in the future, while the old men remain glued to the past, and their memories.

In her small way, Veronica continues that long and extra-ordinary line of women in Fugard's work, women struggling against their disempowerment, who reach a kind of apotheosis

90

in the figure of his mother, Elizabeth Magdalena Potgieter, as the muse of *The Captain's Tiger*, his next work, and the most consciously concerned with memory up to then – the 1998 New York production was subtitled 'A Memoir for the Stage'. In a 1992 *New York Times* interview the playwright had referred, as he often does, to the sustaining power of women in his creative life, from his mother – 'a really frustrated, a silenced woman [who] realized that, through me, she could make a noise' – to Yvonne Bryceland, who spoke through many of his female characters. Beside their affirmative power, however, there is an idealizing or stereotyping of women, even perhaps an element of misogyny, which surfaces, for example, in *Playland*; but the manifest strength, the humour and lack of self-pity of so many female characters, as witnessed by Bryceland, or by the young women of *My Life*, or Esmeralda Biehl (the young Coloured woman cast as Veronica), give substance to the playwright's wish (as he put it in 1992) to identify with the 'unshackling' of the 'gender barrier' that must accompany the breaking-down of race barriers in South Africa.

Yet it is unlikely that *The Captain's Tiger* furthers that unshackling, despite being dedicated to the mother whose photograph as a young woman is displayed as a frontispiece to the printed text, and who comes to life in the play. On the other hand, the play demonstrates once more the surprising power of Fugard's kind of drama, assimilating diverse influences from home and abroad, by using a limited, claustrophobic, almost imprisoning space, in which to take the audience on its journey – or to use its dominant metaphor, its voyage. This is not the first play of Fugard's to be set outside South Africa; but so far there has been only one other that was – *A Place with the Pigs* (1987), set in *'A pigsty, in a village, somewhere in the author's imagination'* (opening stage direction). Despite its evocative shipboard setting, this play could also be said to stand 'somewhere in the author's imagination', suggesting as it does a fantasy recalled, or a Pirandellian dream, in which, for example, the dead can come alive again, a long-dead mother can appear in person, and not just as she was when the young man who remembers her knew her, but also as a figure from *before* he knew her, from before he was born.

To experience memory is akin to experiencing a dreamworld, in which past and present interact, and the past in this play has a presence that is almost frightening, that holds us in an iron grip as it obliges us to attend to its story. This is Fugard as Ancient Mariner (there is a reference to Coleridge's dream-poem in the twelfth of its fifteen scenes, when his ship drifts in the Doldrums).

The Captain's Tiger was the first of Fugard's plays to be premiered (on 5 August 1997) at the newly multiracial State Theatre in Pretoria, where it received mixed reviews: attacked for sentimentality, yet also welcomed for avoiding grandiose gestures about the 'dark past' in favour of trying to come to terms with 'reconciliation, hope and truth'.[12] By contrast, it was greeted with some damning notices in the USA, where one critic remarked that it was 'about as dangerous as a set of dentures [. . .] a nice, safe, old man's play'.[13] But he also referred to it as a 'memory play' – which it is, and as which it should be judged: a kind of drama in which we should expect dramatic conflict and the development of character to be subordinated to narrative and reflection; a kind of drama in which the personal and private are likely to take precedence over the public and social. Hence the whole tone of the play – from the moment that the Author-figure calls attention to himself by ringing the ship's bell at the start, to the conclusion when he rings it again – is retrospective, its dramatic structure circular. To call *The Captain's Tiger* a memory play alerts us to the fact that here we are invited to enter a realm protected from the outside world, in order that we may explore it, through fantasy and dream. As the would-be writer at its centre exclaims to the young mother his imagination has conjured up from her photograph, the imagination has its own kind of freedom: 'Creative authority. That's what you've put your finger on young lady. The freedom and authority of the creative artist to go in any direction his imagination chooses. Theoretically I can do anything I like with you. It's a hell of a responsibility you know' (CT 9). Assisted by his muse and supported by his shipmate, an illiterate Swahili mechanic called Donkeyman, the callow young would-be writer struggles to balance the potential of art, and the need for responsibility, echoing Fugard's personal struggle to come to terms with the conflicting emotions aroused by memories of his mother and the demands of the black man (another surrogate father) who first urged him to 'speak Tiger. Why? Ni uango pia – it is also for me!' (*CT* 74)

Donkeyman's presence, as the silent observer of his young shipmate, then his audience, and finally his challenge, is not without its ironies: the pidgin Swahili Fugard gives him is clumsy and inaccurate, and, despite being corrected in the London production, serves to suggest an unconvincing Caliban to the young Prospero. The older Prospero's presumption in Shakespeare's play is undermined; Fugard's paternalism remains insufficiently questioned, despite Donkeyman's fierce final words: 'You write . . . Bullshit!' (*CT* 74). The man's anger, we are to understand, is prompted by Tiger's decision to throw the novel about his mother overboard – a betrayal of both his own skill, and its usefulness for others. Without any hint of Fugard's future, when he went on to learn a different kind of narrative inscription through collaborating with the black man, the young Fugard/Tiger's attempt to learn Donkeyman's language comes across as too little too late. If we remember that this is all happening in 1952 (Fugard's journey on the *Graigaur* was in fact a year later), we may excuse it. And the more questionable aspects of the proceedings have been reduced in production: for the UK premiere at The Orange Tree, Richmond, London, in 2000, Fugard permitted the use of two actors as his older and younger selves, instead of playing them both himself, as he did in the USA. This created a less indulgent and sentimental tone, while gaining sympathy for his older, manipulative self.

However, to engage with the play's concerns we also need to sympathize with the young Tiger, and his problems of separation and growing up, friendship and loyalty, across class and race divisions. The author's young alter ego is intent upon writing his mother's life story as a paragon of virtue, a 'Karoo woman as Hero [. . .] You and Olive Schreiner' (*CT* 35); and so he creates his muse out of his mother's photo, whose appearance on stage immediately begins to assert its independence as a representation, which, with a neat irony, reminds the putative author of what he has forgotten:

BETTY. I've watched you grow up, standing there in front of me . . . staring . . . staring. You left quite a few grubby fingerprints on the glass to prove it.
You mean you don't remember?

(CT 7)

The young author insists that his memory must dictate what he writes, whatever she might feel about it. But his mother-muse rebels, and creates her own reality, which he must accept; including the reality of his crippled father, who, once again, comes between the white youth and his black servant-friend: 'I can't make a happy ending out of my Dad' (CT 73), he finally exclaims, echoing Hally in '*Master Harold*' as he despairingly throws his manuscript overboard, to the dismay of both Betty and Donkeyman.

Clearly, Fugard has yet to confront his father. In *The Captain's Tiger*, Donkeyman takes on the paternal role of initiating the young man into adulthood (an embarrasingly stereotyped sequence); but the real interest of the play centres on his mother's influence and memory. One of its most telling moments occurs during a dream, when she arrives like a succubus, hovering seductively over his sleeping form, and he says, 'That does it. I'm putting on the light.' And she replies, 'You can't. You're powerless. You can't move' (CT 46). He is caught in the grip of memory, as strong as a dream. 'Waves of desire are passing over me,' his mother-muse says, caressing herself, before sliding in beside him (CT 46–9). It is as if the Oedipal ambivalence of the young aspiring writer's feelings can be realized only in that safe place where writers explore what is taboo – in their art, which means, for Fugard, on stage.

For many South Africans, it is the past that has been taboo: an area of personal sin and social trauma, from which they would like to imagine they have escaped, but which haunts them as never before. Their yearning for restitution is as powerful as the reminders of suffering and shame that mark both private and public life. It is a tribute to Fugard that, despite his removal from the country, he continues to try and write himself into its ongoing script, although with sometimes debateable success. As he puts it, 'I have made a discovery bewilderingly late in life: how free a medium the stage really

94

is, and how infinite the possibilities of storytelling. The new South Africa involves liberation on many levels. I want to deal myself into that freedom.'[14]

Freeing himself up from the demand to bear witness to the present seems to have brought with it a need to bear witness to the past – or at least, the personal past, through memory. Hence his next, and most recent play, *Sorrows and Rejoicings*, in which a trio of women offer their remembrances of the dead main character, ex-activist-writer Dawid Olivier from the Karoo. The play was premiered 4 May 2001 at the McCarter Theater in Princeton, New Jersey, before appearing in New York, Cape Town and (in 2002) London. The American response was generally negative, one 'jaundiced South African journalist' writing that she found the US production dated and static, 'an opera without music', moreover accusing the playwright of having effectively 'gagged' the women in the play; a less jaundiced South African journalist who saw the Cape Town production later the same year found it 'poignant' and 'rewarding', and admired its 'stately, contrapuntal eloquence'.[15]

Significantly, both reviewers sensed the importance of music as an underlying structural device, touching on something fundamental to Fugard's sense of what makes drama, the way its rhythms reveal the emotional truths that lie beneath the surface of the words. As he observed in *Cousins*: 'I try to write plays with the same emotional dynamic, the same organization of energy as there is in music' (C. 37). *Sorrows and Rejoicings* takes to an extreme the tendency in all his work of characters' voices to become a series of interweaving monologues, often on different planes of consciousness or reality, rather than a mere interchange of dialogue. In making this more apparent – dangerously so, for audiences attuned to a more conventional theatre experience – *Sorrows and Rejoicings* expresses the meaning of memory in terms of linked utterances, one of them from beyond the grave, as the characters speak themselves like arias, rather than engaging with each other. Fugard's hero (played in Cape Town and London by Marius Weyers, his Dimetos) is an Afrikaner poet who rejected apartheid in the 1980s and left the country on a one-way 'exit permit', but who has returned after years of fruitless exile to die in his home village. The play opens as the three women in his life return

95

after his funeral: his ex-wife Allison, the liberal-minded 'English girl from the city'; his ex-lover Marta, the Afrikaans-speaking Coloured servant from the location; and his illegitimate child by Marta, Rebecca, who stands and watches the other two from the doorway for most of the play, until her moment to bear witness arrives, and she accuses her mother of being the mere ghost of a servant 'looking after her dead masters and madams', and her father of having created her, the 'spook kind' (freak child), as his only contribution to 'the new South Africa' (*SR* 41).

Unlike the starry-eyed Veronica of *Valley Song*, this resentful teenager seems to stand as a warning of continuing hatred and violence, as well as a reminder of all the rejected and orphaned children of South Africa. She has destroyed the poems that her father's wife Allison wants to publish as a memorial entitled *Rejoicings*, thus leaving us with the *Sorrows* of the title – an allusion to the exiled Ovid's *Tristia*, and an expression of what home feels like for the returnee, expressed by Dawid's last monologue in bitter praise of the Karoo, using (once again, as in *The Guest*) Eugène Marais's vision of South Africa as a land that 'gives nothing, but demands everything. Tears, the names of the dead, the widow's lament, the pleading gestures and cries of children . . .' (*SR* 53). And yet reconciliation if not forgiveness has taken place, embodied by the concluding gesture of the play, as Rebecca and Marta leave together. In his own way, which has become ever more obviously what it always was, that of a creator of small-scale plays touching on ever larger themes, Fugard reminds us of the importance of memory, from which we derive not only our morality, but our identity. In a country in which, as the central character of *Sorrows and Rejoicings* says, time is 'a hungry rat' (*SR* 16) gnawing away at us, memory, and its public face, history, remain irreplaceable.

Fugard's 'post-apartheid' plays are perhaps bound to express pathos and loss rather than anger and defiance, which suggests they may be of less importance in the present than his earlier work. But, as always with Fugard, considered in terms of the changing context of South African realities as well as his personal position, things are not so simple. The representation of the fear of the other – if anything, the issue of our time worldwide – continues as a central theme, as does the struggle to retrieve some element of hope for the future, after the startling and dramatic changes in his country. To many South Africans, he appears to have sidelined himself from their daily concerns: the concerns of poverty, violence and disease, which have taken over from the horrors of apartheid. Bearing witness as a function of social responsibility seems to have been replaced by a kind of personal witnessing as a function of individual moral responsibility. But have these aspects of his work ever been entirely absent, or separate? I do not think so. That does not mean that Fugard is beyond criticism, far from it. As in T. S. Eliot's 'Little Gidding', 'every attempt' of his to create new work is a 'new beginning, a raid on the inarticulate' with deteriorating equipment; and, as he grows older, the 'pattern' of the living and the dead grows 'more complicated'. At the heart of the pattern for Fugard is that moment he touched on in his memoir *Cousins*, when recalling the confession to him of his homosexuality by 'bad' cousin Garth, a confession that remains a kind of touchstone for a director trying to help actors 'embrace their own personal moment of truth'. Fugard's own moment of truth arrived with the realization that, even as a boy, he already knew on some level what Garth confessed to him, and the thrilling 'sense of power' the discovery produced in him. That is 'my real territory as a dramatist: the world of secrets, with their powerful effect on human behaviour and the trauma of their revelation' (*C.* 74).

What he also realized was the ambiguous power of the creator, which may, in works like *Sizwe Bansi* or *The Island*, *The Blood Knot/Blood Knot* or *Boesman and Lena* or '*Master Harold*' ... *and the Boys*, invest the simplest and most humble people and events with significance, thereby liberating us all at least momentarily from our sufferings, our mortal condition; but which can also imprison and destroy under the load of trauma and angst it carries, as happens in what Fugard himself calls in retrospect his 'literary breakdowns', *Orestes*, *Dimetos* and *A Place with the Pigs* (*C.* 89). Searching for his own truth as he explores the truths of others, Fugard invests his drama with a challenge to us to do the same. What further revelations are in store for us in later instalments of the work of the master of Nieu Bethesda?

Notes

INTRODUCTION

1. Njabulo Ndebele, *Rediscovery of the Ordinary* (Fordsburg, Johannesburg: Congress of South African Writers, 1991), 37–57.
2. See Albie Sachs, 'Preparing Ourselves for Freedom', repr. in *Spring is Rebellious: Arguments about Cultural Freedom by Albie Sachs and Respondents*, ed. Ingrid de Kok and Karen Press (Cape Town: buchu books, 1990), 19.
3. See e.g. Albert Wertheim, *The Dramatic Art of Athol Fugard: From South Africa to the World* (Bloomington: Indiana University Press, 2000), whose chapters on the Township Plays cannot avoid their politics.
4. Athol Fugard, Foreword, in *Plays: One* (London: Faber & Faber, 1998).
5. Charles Fourie, 'Interview with the Outsider', *Electronic Mail & Guardian* (14 Aug. 1997), http://www.mg.co.za/art/reviews/97aug-captains_tiger.html.
6. Brian Crow and Chris Banfield, *An Introduction to Post-Colonial Theatre* (Cambridge: Cambridge University Press, 1996), 101; Helen Gilbert and Joanne Tompkins, *Post-Colonial Drama: Theory, Practice, Politics* (London: Routledge, 1996), 41–2.
7. John Peter, 'The Island', *Sunday Times, Culture* (30 Jan. 2000), 24.
8. Dennis Walder, 'A Voice for the Afrikaner? Interview with Athol Fugard' (1996), in Marcia Blumberg and Dennis Walder (eds.), *South African Theatre As/And Intervention* (Amsterdam: Rodopi, 1999), 220.
9. Athol Fugard, 'Fugard on Acting', *Theatre Quarterly*, 8/28 (Winter 1977–8), 84.
10. Quoted in Ursula Barnett, *A Vision of Order: A Study of Black South African Literature in English (1914–1980)* (London: Sinclair Browne, 1983), 228.

11. Mary Benson, 'Athol Fugard and "One Little Corner of the World"', *Yale/Theatre*, 4 (Winter 1973), 55.
12. Athol Fougard [*sic*], 'The Blood Knot' (foreword to an extract), *Contrast* (Cape Town), 2/1 (Autumn 1962), 29.
13. T. R. H. Davenport, Preface, in *The Transfer of Power in South Africa* (Cape Town: David Philip, 1998), p. vii.

CHAPTER 1. PROTEST AND SURVIVAL

1. Craig Raine, 'An Interview with Athol Fugard', *Quarto*, 9 (Aug. 1980), 9.
2. Ibid.
3. Nadine Gordimer, 'English-Language Literature and Politics in South Africa', in C. Heywood (ed.), *Aspects of South African Literature* (London: Heinemann, 1976), 110.
4. Sheila Fugard, 'The Apprenticeship Years', *Twentieth Century Literature: Athol Fugard Special Issue*, ed. Jack Barbera, 39 (Winter 1993), 398.
5. Jonathan Marks, 'Interview with Athol Fugard', *Yale/Theatre*, 4 (Winter 1973), 72; anon.,'Afrikaner Humanist' (profile), *Observer*, 18 July 1971.
6. Sheila Fugard, 'The Apprenticeship Years', 405.
7. Almeda K. Rae, 'Athol Fugard, Barney Simon' (interviews), in Stephen Gray (ed.), *Athol Fugard* (Johannesburg: McGraw-Hill, 1982), 51–2.
8. Athol Fugard, personal interview, 'The Ashram', Sardinia Bay, 3 Jan. 1982.
9. See Randolph Vigne, *Liberals against Apartheid: A History of the Liberal Party of South Africa* (London: Macmillan, 2000).
10. See Heinrich von Staden, 'An Interview with Athol Fugard', *Theater*, 14 (Winter 1982), 42.
11. Athol Fugard, 'The Gift of Freedom', in Richard Findlater (ed.), *At the Royal Court: 25 Years of the English Stage Company* (Derbyshire: Amber Lane, 1981), 160.
12. Peter Wilhelm, 'Athol Fugard at Forty' (interview), *To the Point* (Johannesburg), 3 June 1972, repr. in Gray (ed.), *Athol Fugard*, 109–14, at 114.

CHAPTER 2. PLAYS OF PLACE

1. Fugard continued revising the play after its premiere, until finally, for the twenty-fifth anniversary production at the Yale

Repertory Theatre, New Haven (subsequently in New York), in 1985, he used the substantially reduced text, retitled *Blood Knot* (the main alteration was to cut Morrie's long speeches). Unless otherwise indicated, text references are to the revised version, as first and solely published in my edition of *Selected Plays* (Oxford: Oxford University Press, 1987), and in a new edition as *Port Elizabeth Plays* (Oxford: Oxford University Press, 2000).

2. Albert Camus, *The Rebel* (1951), trans. Anthony Bower (1953; Harmondsworth: Penguin, 1977), 108–9.

3. Athol Fugard, 'Introduction', in *Boesman and Lena and other Plays* (Cape Town: Oxford University Press, 1980), p. ix. These (and other) words were later silently revised for the publication of Fugard's *Notebooks*, ed. Mary Benson (see N. 9 ff). I give this as the original.

4. Ibid., p. viii.

5. Mary Benson, *Athol Fugard and Barney Simon* (Randburg: Ravan Press, 1997), 4–5.

6. Roger Omond, *The Apartheid Handbook: A Guide to South Africa's Everyday Racial Policies* (Harmondsworth: Penguin Books, 1985), 2–4.

7. See Michael Ignatieff, *The Warrior's Honour: Ethnic War and the Modern Conscience* (London: Chatto & Windus, 1998).

8. Loren Kruger, *The Drama of South Africa: Plays, Pageants and Publics since 1910* (London: Routledge, 1999), 109.

9. Bernard Levin, 'They Really Are Blind', *Daily Mail*, 22 Feb. 1963. This was in response to the New Arts, Hampstead, London production, with Ian Bannen as Morris and Zakes Mokae as Zach.

10. Stanley Kauffman, 'Boesman and Lena', *New Republic*, 25 July 1970, 16.

11. Errol Durbach, ' "No Time for Apartheid": Dancing Free of the System in Athol Fugard's *Boesman and Lena*', in Marcia Blumberg and Dennis Walder (eds.), *South African Theatre As/And Intervention* (Amsterdam: Rodopi, 1999), 67. As Blumberg points out, Lena in fact speaks of areas where her racial group could stay, but she has been unable to: 'Languages of Violence: Fugard's *Boesman and Lena*', in James Redmond (ed.), *Violence in Drama* (Cambridge: Cambridge University Press, 1991), 240.

12. Russell Vandenbroucke, *Truths the Hand Can Touch: The Theatre of Athol Fugard* (New York: Theatre Communications Group, 1985), 70–4.

13. There is some uncertainty about the dating of these entries, which were revised from their originals by Mary Benson for her edition of the *Notebooks*.

CHAPTER 3. TOWNSHIP WITNESSING

1. Mongane Serote, 'Art as Craft and Politics: Theatre' (1986), in Serote, *On the Horizon* (Fordsburg, Johannesburg: Congress of South African Writers, 1990), 45.
2. Laura Jones, *Nothing Except Ourselves: The Harsh Times and Bold Theater of South Africa's Mbongeni Ngema* (New York: Viking Penguin, 1994), 38.
3. Milan Kundera, *The Book of Laughter and Forgetting* (London: Faber & Faber, 1992), 3.
4. Benjamin Pogrund, 'Nights When *Tsotsi* Was Born', *Rand Daily Mail*, 11 Feb. 1980, 9; Anthony Sampson, *Drum* (London: Collins, 1956), 228.
5. R.G., 'A European Looks at *No-Good Friday* and Finds It Good Theatre', *Zonk* (Dec. 1958), 55.
6. Bloke Modisane, *Blame Me On History* (Harmondsworth: Penguin, 1990), 289–91.
7. Mary Benson, 'Keeping an Appointment with the Future', *Theatre Quarterly*, 7 (Winter 1977–8), 78.
8. Barrie Hough, 'Interview with Fugard', 30 Nov. 1977, repr. in Stephen Gray (ed.), *Athol Fugard* (Johannesburg: McGraw-Hill, 1982), 122.
9. Lewis Nkosi, 'Let's Vitalise the Theatre', *Contact* (Cape Town), 27 June 1959, 11.
10. See Robert Kavanagh, *Theatre and Cultural Struggle in South Africa* (London: Zed Books, 1985), 161; and Dennis Walder, 'Resituating Fugard: South African Drama as Witness', *New Theatre Quarterly*, 8/32 (Nov. 1992), especially 349.
11. See Dennis Walder, 'Introduction', in Athol Fugard, *The Township Plays* (Oxford: Oxford University Press, 2000), pp. xxv–xxvi.
12. Dori Laub, 'An Event without a Witness: Truth, Testimony and Survival', in Shoshana Feldman and Dori Laub (eds.), *Testimony: Crises of Witnessing in Literature, Pyschoanalysis, and History* (London: Routledge, 1992), 76.
13. Athol Fugard, 'When Brecht and Sizwe Bansi Met in New Brighton', *Observer*, 8 Aug. 1982, 31.
14. Ibid.
15. George Steiner, *Antigones: The Antigone Myth in Western Literature, Art and Thought* (Oxford: Oxford University Press, 1986), 144.
16. Dale Lautenbach, 'An Island of Dreams', *Weekend Argus*, Cape Town, 2 Nov. 1985.
17. John Kani and Winston Ntshona, interviewed by Peter Rosenwald, 'Separate Fables', *Guardian*, 8 Jan. 1974, 10.

18. Justin Pearce, 'Visions of a Rainbow Culture', *Mail & Guardian*, 21 July 1995.

CHAPTER 4. CARNAL REALITIES

1. Athol Fugard, personal interview, 'The Ashram', Sardinia Bay, 3 Jan. 1982; personal correspondence, 5 June 1976; personal interview, London, 20 Feb. 1996.
2. 'Athol Fugard', interview with A. Christopher Tucker, *Transatlantic Review*, 53/4 (1976), 87.
3. P. W. Botha, quoted in Roger Omond, *The Apartheid Handbook: A Guide to South Africa's Everyday Racial Policies* (Harmondsworth: Penguin, 1985), 26. And see *TP* 273 n. to p. 91.
4. Jeanne Colleran, 'Re-Situating Fugard: Re-Thinking Revolutionary Theatre', *South African Theatre Journal*, 9 (Sept. 1995), 47–8.
5. Brian Astbury, *The Space/Die Ruimte/Indawo* (Cape Town: Moyra and Azriel Fine, n.d.), no page nos.
6. 'Honesty, Integrity, but Dulness in Play', *Argus*, 29 Mar. 1972.
7. Elsa Joubert, 'Immorality Drama', *Rapport*, Johannesburg, 2 Apr. 1972, trans. J. Janisch; Robert Cushman, 'The Naked Truth', *Observer*, 27 Jan. 1974; both repr. in Stephen Gray (ed.), *Athol Fugard* (Johannesburg: McGraw-Hill, 1982), 85–8.
8. John Elsom, 'The Coloured', *Listener*, 31 Jan. 1974, 159.
9. Albert Camus, *Notebooks: 1935–1942*, trans. Philip Thody, first published in English as *Carnets 1935–1942* (London: Hamish Hamilton, 1963; New York: Marlowe & Company, 1996), 136.
10. See Richard Whitaker, 'Dimoetes to Dimetos: The Evolution of a Myth', *English Studies in Africa*, 24/1 (1981), 45–59.
11. Athol Fugard, Programme Note, *Dimetos* (Edinburgh: Edinburgh International Festival, 1975).
12. Personal interview with Yvonne Bryceland, London, 21 Sept. 1983.
13. Michael Billington, 'Dimetos', *Guardian*, 29 Aug. 1975, 10.
14. John Elsom, 'The True and False Pilgrim', *Listener*, 4 Sept. 1975, 311–12.
15. Derek Wilson, 'Powerful Fugard Play Gets Deserved Airing', *Argus*, Supplement, 28 Dec. 1981, 3.
16. See Michael Rustin, *The Good Society and the Inner World: Psychoanalysis, Poltics and Culture* (London: Verso, 1991), 197.
17. Leonard Thompson, *A History of South Africa*, rev. edn. (New Haven: Yale University Press, 1995), 215.

18. Albert Memmi, *The Colonizer and the Colonized* (1957), introduction by J.-P. Sartre, trans. Howard Greenfield (London: Souvenir Press, 1974), 19 ff.

CHAPTER 5. MEMORY PLAYS

1. See Esther Leslie, *Walter Benjamin: Overpowering Conformism* (London: Pluto Press, 2000), 82. See also my essay, ' "The Fitful Muse": Fugard's Plays of Memory', *The European Legacy*, 7, 6 (2002), 697–708, on which I have drawn for this chapter.
2. Mel Gussow, 'Notes . . . on *"Master Harold"* ', *New York Times*, 21 Mar. 1982, 4.
3. Albert Wertheim, *The Dramatic Art of Athol Fugard: From South Africa to the World* (Bloomington: Indiana University Press, 2000), 136.
4. Joseph Lelyveld, *New York Times*, 24 Mar. 1983, 16.
5. Personal interview with Mary Benson and Ross Devenish (17 Dec. 1982), who also said the initial prompt was a letter from Sam Semela to Fugard when the playwright's mother died.
6. Interview with Paul Allen, 'Kaleidoscope' (BBC Radio 4), 25 Jan. 1984.
7. Errol Durbach, ' *"Master Harold"* . . . *and the Boys*: Athol Fugard and the Psychopathology of Apartheid', *Modern Drama*, 30/4 (1987), 512.
8. Alisa Solomon, ' "Look at History": An Interview with Zakes Mokae', *Theater*, 14 (Winter 1982), 28–9.
9. The most forceful critique of the play was made by Nicholas Visser, 'Drama and Politics in a State of Emergency: *My Children! My Africa!*', *Twentieth Century Literature: Athol Fugard Issue*, ed. Jack Barbera, 39/4 (Winter 1993), 486–502.
10. Raeford Daniel, 'Athol Fugard – and All the Fun of the Fair', *Weekly Mail*, 24 July 1992, 30.
11. Athol Fugard, 'A Voice for the Afrikaner?' (1996), in M. Blumberg and D. Walder (eds.), *South African Theatre As/And Intervention* (Amsterdam: Rodopi, 1999), 220.
12. Elliott Makhaya, 'Fugard Finishes New Play', *The Sowetan*, 1 May 1997, 7.
13. Joel Beers, 'This Tiger's Got No Bite', *Orange County Weekly*, 14 Feb. 1999, http://www.ocweekly.com/ink/archives/98/46the-072498-beers.shtm.
14. Qtd Guy Willoughby, 'Freeing Fugard', *Mail & Guardian* (24–30 August 2001), 5.

15. Christina Scott, 'Fugard's work of contradiction', *Daily Mail & Guardian* (25 May 2001), at http//www.mg.co.za/mg/art/theatre/0105/010525-fugard.html; Guy Willoughby, 'Portrait of a writer', *Daily Mail & Guardian* (7 Sept. 2001), at http//www.mg.co.za/mg/art/2001/2001sep/010907.

Select Bibliography

WORKS BY FUGARD

Published Plays

The early works are now generally available only in collections.

The Blood Knot: A Play in Seven Scenes (Johannesburg: Simondium, 1963; New York: Odyssey Press, 1964).

Hello and Goodbye: A Play in Two Acts (Cape Town: Balkema, 1966; New York: S. French, 1971; London: Oxford University Press, 1973).

Boesman and Lena: A Play in Two Acts (Cape Town: Buren, 1969; New York: S. French, 1971; London: Oxford University Press, 1973).

People Are Living There: A Play in Two Acts (Cape Town: Buren, 1969; London: Oxford University Press, 1970; New York: S. French, 1970).

The Coat: Athol Fugard; The Third Degree: Don Maclennan: Two Experiments in Play-Making (Cape Town: Balkema, 1971).

Sizwe Bansi Is Dead: Complete Text, by Athol Fugard, John Kani and Winston Ntshona (London: Hansom Books, 1973).

A Lesson from Aloes (Oxford: Oxford University Press, 1981; New York: Random House, 1981).

'Master Harold' . . . and the Boys (New York: Knopf, 1982; Oxford: Oxford University Press, 1983).

The Road to Mecca: A Play in Two Acts (London: Faber & Faber, 1985).

A Place with the Pigs: A Personal Parable (London: Faber & Faber, 1988).

My Children! My Africa! (New York: S. French, 1990; London: Faber & Faber, 1990).

Playland . . . and Other Words (Johannesburg: Witwatersrand University Press, 1992); republished as *Playland* (London: Faber & Faber, 1993; New York: S. French, 1994).

Valley Song (London: Faber & Faber, 1996).

The Captain's Tiger (Johannesburg: Witwatersrand University Press, 1997); republished as *The Captain's Tiger: A Memoir for the Stage* (New York: S. French, 1999).

Sorrows and Rejoicings (New York: Theatre Communications Group, 2002).

Screenplays

The Occupation, unperformed camera script (1964), in *My Children! My Africa! and Selected Shorter Plays*, ed. Stephen Gray (Johannesburg: Witwatersrand University Press, 1990).

Mille Miglia, for TV (1968), in *My Children! My Africa! and Selected Shorter Plays*, ed. Stephen Gray (Johannesburg: Witwatersrand University Press, 1990).

The Guest: An Episode in the Life of Eugène Marais, by Athol Fugard and Ross Devenish (Johannesburg: Ad. Donker, 1977), in *Interior Plays*, ed. Dennis Walder (Oxford: Oxford University Press, 2000).

Marigolds in August and *The Guest: Two Screenplays*, by Athol Fugard and Ross Devenish (New York: Theatre Communications Group, 1992).

Collections

Statements: Three Plays, by Athol Fugard, John Kani, and Winston Ntshona (London: Oxford University Press, 1974; New York: Theatre Communications Group, 1986). Contains *Sizwe Bansi Is Dead*, *The Island* and *Statements after an Arrest under the Immorality Act*, with a useful introduction by Athol Fugard.

Dimetos and Two Early Plays (Oxford: Oxford University Press, 1977). Contains *Dimetos*, *Nongogo* and *No-Good Friday*.

Boesman and Lena and Other Plays (Oxford: Oxford University Press, 1978). Contains *The Blood Knot*, *People Are Living There*, *Hello and Goodbye* and *Boesman and Lena*, with a useful introduction by Athol Fugard.

Selected Plays, ed. Dennis Walder (Oxford: Oxford University Press, 1987). Contains *'Master Harold' . . . and the Boys*, *Blood Knot* (new version), *Hello and Goodbye* and *Boesman and Lena*, with a full introduction, notes and glossary by Dennis Walder, republished as *Port Elizabeth Plays* (Oxford: Oxford University Press, 2000), with a new preface by Athol Fugard. The first collection edited to scholarly standards.

My Children! My Africa! and Selected Shorter Plays, ed. Stephen Gray (Johannesburg: Witwatersrand University Press, 1990). Contains *My Children! My Africa!*, *The Occupation*, *The Coat*, *Mille Miglia*, *Orestes* (in the form of a descriptive letter) and *The Drummer*, with a short introduction by Stephen Gray.

The Township Plays, ed. Dennis Walder (Oxford: Oxford University Press, 1993). Contains *No-Good Friday*, *Nongogo*, *The Coat*, *Sizwe*

Bansi Is Dead and *The Island*, with a full introduction, notes and glossary by Dennis Walder, republished 2000, with a new preface by Athol Fugard. The second collection edited to scholarly standards, uniform with *The Port Elizabeth Plays*.

Plays: One (London: Faber & Faber, 1998). Contains *The Road to Mecca, A Place with the Pigs, My Children! My Africa!, Playland* and *Valley Song*, with a brief Foreword by Athol Fugard.

Interior Plays, ed. Dennis Walder (Oxford: Oxford University Press, 2000). Contains *People Are Living There, Statements after an Arrest under the Immorality Act, Dimetos, The Guest* and *A Lesson from Aloes*, with a full introduction, notes and glossary by Dennis Walder, and a preface by Athol Fugard. The third collection edited to scholarly standards, uniform with *The Port Elizabeth Plays* and *The Township Plays*.

Other Works

Tsotsi (Johannesburg: Quagga Press/Ad. Donker, 1980; London: Rex Collings, 1980; New York: Random House, 1980). Fugard's long unpublished novel, written 1959–60.

Notebooks: 1960–1977, ed. Mary Benson (Johannesburg: Ad. Donker, 1983; London: Faber & Faber, 1983; New York: Knopf, 1984). A vital resource, despite haphazard editing.

Cousins: A Memoir (Johannesburg: Witwatersrand University Press, 1994; New York: Theatre Communications Group, 1997). The first volume of memoirs.

Feature Films

Boesman and Lena, motion picture, Bluewater Productions, 1974.

The Guest at Steenkampskraal, in collaboration with Ross Devenish, motion picture, BBC2 Film International, 5 Mar. 1977, later released as *The Guest*.

Marigolds in August, in collaboration with Ross Devenish, motion picture, Serpent Southern production, Johannesburg Film Festival, April 1980.

The Road to Mecca, in collaboration with Peter Goldsmid, motion picture, Ultimate Films, National Festival of the Arts, Grahamstown, July 1991.

Articles

'*Orestes* Reconstructed: A Letter to an American Friend', *Theatre Quarterly*, 8/32 (1979), 3–6, repr. in *My Children! My Africa! and*

Selected Shorter Plays, ed. Stephen Gray (Johannesburg: Witwatersrand University Press, 1990). The only publicly available version of this experimental work.

'Some Problems of a Playwright from South Africa', *Twentieth Century Literature*, 39 (Winter 1993), 381–93. Edited transcript of a talk given at New York University, 16 Oct. 1990.

'Recent Notebook Entries', *Twentieth Century Literature*, 39 (Winter 1993), 526–36.

Interviews

Fugard has always been a generous interviewee, thus only a selection of the most pointed and/or substantial are here cited, in order of appearance.

Marks, Jonathan, 'Interview with Athol Fugard', *Yale/Theatre*, 4 (Winter 1973), 64-72.

Benson, Mary, 'Athol Fugard and "One Little Corner of the World" ', *Yale/Theatre*, 4 (Winter 1973), 55–62.

Bragg, Melvyn, 'Athol Fugard, Playwright', *Listener*, 5 Dec. 1974, 734–5.

Benson, Mary, 'Keeping an Appointment with the Future', *Theatre Quarterly*, 7 (Winter 1977–8), 77-83.

Raine, Craig, 'An Interview with Athol Fugard', *Quarto*, 9 (Aug. 1980), 9–14.

Von Staden, Heinrich, 'An Interview with Athol Fugard', *Theater*, 14 (Winter 1982), 41–6.

Gussow, Mel, 'Profiles: Witness: Athol Fugard', *New Yorker*, 20 Dec. 1982, 47–94.

Rae, Almeda K., 'Athol Fugard, Barney Simon: "The Family Plays of the Sixties" ', in Stephen Gray (ed.), *Athol Fugard* (Johannesburg: McGraw-Hill, 1982), 40–52.

Honegger, Gita, et al., 'An Interview with Athol Fugard', *Theater*, 16 (Fall/Winter 1984), 33–9.

Richards, Lloyd, 'The Art of Theater VIII: Athol Fugard', *Paris Review*, 31 (1989), 129–51.

Henry III, William A., 'On the Front Line of Anger', *Time*, 7 Aug. 1989, 56–8.

Riordan, Rory, 'Athol Fugard', *Crux*, 25 (Feb. 1991), 3–14.

van Niekerk, Phillip, 'Fears and Loathing of a Liberated Old White South African Titan', *Observer*, 1 Jan. 1995, 18.

Baitz, Jon Robin, and Fugard, Athol, 'On South Africa and Hope: A Dialogue', *New York Times*, 10 Dec. 1995, II: 1, 4.

Walder, Dennis, 'A Voice for the Afrikaner?' (1996), in Marcia Blumberg and Dennis Walder (eds.), *South African Theatre As/And Intervention* (Amsterdam: Rodopi, 1999), 219–30.

Goodwin, Christopher, 'White Man without the Burden', *Sunday Times*, News Review, 16 Jan. 2000, 4.

Willoughby, Guy, 'Freeing Fugard', *Mail & Guardian*, 24–30 July 2001, 5.

BIBLIOGRAPHY

Read, John, *Athol Fugard: A Bibliography* (Grahamstown: National English Literary Museum, 1991).

http://www.iainfisher.com/atholpst.html useful web site.

CRITICISM

Books

Gray, Stephen (ed.), *Athol Fugard* (Johannesburg: McGraw-Hill, 1982). Contains valuable background material, interviews, reviews and a selection of criticism.

Orkin, Martin, *Drama and the South African State* (Johannesburg: Witwatersrand University Press; Manchester: Manchester University Press, 1991). Ground-breaking study drawing on Cultural Materialist approaches to analyse theatre in terms of dissidence, opposition, and hegemony.

Vandenbroucke, Russell, *Truths the Hand Can Touch: The Theatre of Athol Fugard* (New York: Theatre Communications Group, 1985). The 'universalist' approach, with valuable biographical material.

Walder, Dennis, *Selected Plays of Fugard* (London: Longman York Press, 1980). Brief annotated introduction to *Sizwe Bansi is Dead*, *The Island* and *Statements after an Arrest under the Immorality Act* as political plays.

—— *Athol Fugard* (Basingstoke: Macmillan, 1984). Account of the life and work up to 1982, emphasizing Fugard's focus upon his defining staged image, in the contemporary South African context.

Wertheim, Albert, *The Dramatic Art of Athol Fugard: From South Africa to the World* (Bloomington: Indiana University Press, 2000). Enthusiastic 'universalist' account of all the plays up to *The Captain's Tiger*, emphasizing their dramatic shape and motifs.

111

Articles and Book Chapters

Amato, Rob, 'Fugard's Confessional Analysis: *"Master Harold"* . . . *and the Boys'*, in M. J. Daymond, J. U. Jacobs, and M. Lenta (eds.), *Momentum: On Recent South African Writing* (Pietermaritzburg: University of Natal Press, 1984), 198–214. Insightful.

Benson, Mary, 'Athol Fugard and the Eastern Cape', in her *A Far Cry: The Making of a South African* (New York: Viking, 1989; London: Penguin, 1990), 186–205. Unique contextual material by close friend and confidante of Fugard's during the 1960s and later.

Blumberg, Marcia, 'Negotiating the In-Between: Fugard's *Valley Song'*, *Journal of Literary Studies*, 12 (Dec. 1996), 456–69. Focuses on the 'engendering of Veronica's voice' alongside the issue of land ownership.

—— 'Re-Staging Resistance, Re-Viewing Women: 1990s Productions of Fugard's *Hello and Goodbye* and *Boesman and Lena'*, in Jeanne Colleran and Jenny S. Spencer (eds.), *Staging Resistance: Essays on Political Theater* (Ann Arbor: University of Michigan Press, 1998), 123–45. Important feminist critique.

Colleran, Jeanne, 'A Place with the Pigs: Athol Fugard's Afrikaner Parable', *Modern Drama*, 33 (1990), 17–36. One of the few useful analyses of this work.

—— 'Athol Fugard and the Problematics of the Liberal Critique', *Modern Drama*, 38 (1995), 389–407. Important analysis of the US reception of Fugard.

Crow, Brian, 'Athol Fugard', in Bruce King (ed.), *Post-Colonial English Drama: Commonwealth Drama since 1960* (Basingstoke: Macmillan, 1992), 150–64. Broad survey of Fugard's work as dramatizing the self.

Durbach, Errol, ' *"Master Harold"* . . . *and the Boys*: Athol Fugard and the Psychopathology of Apartheid', *Modern Drama*, 30/4 (1987), 505–13. Informed analysis from socio-psychological viewpoint.

—— 'Dancing Free of the System in Athol Fugard's *Boesman and Lena'*, in Marcia Blumberg and Dennis Walder (eds.), *South African Theatre As/And Intervention* (Amsterdam: Rodopi, 1999), 61–74. Argues that exposing apartheid has continuing validity.

Foley, Andrew, 'Fugard, Liberalism, and the Ending of Apartheid', *Current Writing*, 9/2 (1997), 57–75. Reasserting the relevance of Fugard's liberalism in the 'post-apartheid' period.

Gray, Stephen, 'The Coming into Print of Athol Fugard's *Tsotsi'*, *Journal of Commonwealth Literature*, 16 (Aug. 1981), 56–63.

—— 'Athol Fugard's *"Insubstantial Pageant"*: *The Road to Mecca'*, *Australasian Drama Studies*, 7 (Aug. 1985), 45–52. Informed and insightful.

Green, Michael, ' "The Politics of Loving": Fugard and the Metropolis', *English Academy Review*, 2 (1984) 41–54. Raising the issue of overseas versus local reactions.

Kavanagh, Robert, ' "No-Man's Land": Fugard and the Black Intellectuals', in his *Theatre and Cultural Struggle in South Africa* (London: Zed, 1985), 59–83. Marxist account of early Fugard plays in the black South African context.

Kruger, Loren, 'Spaces and Markets', in Kruger, *The Drama of South Africa: Plays, Pageants and Publics since 1910* (London: Routledge, 1999), 154–70. Cultural Materialist account of *Sizwe Bansi* and *The Island* in black performance context in South Africa.

Munro, Margaret, 'The Fertility of Despair: Fugard's Bitter Aloes', *Meanjin*, 40 (Dec. 1981), 472–9. Excellent example of criticism from Australia, where most of Fugard's plays have been produced and well received.

Post, Robert M., 'Racism in Athol Fugard's "Master Harold" . . . and the Boys', *World Literature Written in English*, 30/1 (1990), 97–102. Critical account of the play's approach to this issue.

Seymour, Hilary, 'Sizwe Bansi is Dead: A Study of Artistic Ambivalance', *Race and Class*, 21/3 (1980), 273–289. Questioning political motivation of key Fugard collaborative play.

Visser, Nicholas, 'Drama and Politics in a State of Emergency: Athol Fugard's *My Children! My Africa!*', *Twentieth Century Literature: Athol Fugard Issue*, ed. Jack Barbera, 39/4 (Winter 1993), 486–502. Informed and cogent attack upon Fugard's politics in turning-point play.

Walder, Dennis, 'Resituating Fugard: South African Drama as Witness', *New Theatre Quarterly*, 8/32 (Nov. 1992), 343–61. Questioning survey of Fugard criticism in changing South African context, and an account of more recent plays as 'witness'.

——— 'Questions from a White Man Who Listens: The Voices of *Valley Song*', in Marcia Blumberg and Dennis Walder (eds.), *South African Theatre As/And Intervention* (Amsterdam: Rodopi, 1999), 101–12. Arguing for continuing but qualified relevance of *Valley Song*.

Whitaker, Richard, 'Dimoetos to Dimetos: The Evolution of a Myth', *English Studies in Africa*, 24/1 (1981), 45–59. Analyses the literary and classical origins of the *Dimetos* story.

BACKGROUND READING

Chapman, Michael, *Southern African Literatures* (Harlow Longman, 1996). Massive, wide-ranging and explicitly committed to a 'progressive' agenda; the first study of its kind, displacing all earlier, more limited surveys.

Davis, Geoffrey, and Fuchs, Anne (eds.), *Theatre and Change in South Africa* (Amsterdam: Harwood, 1996). Wide-ranging collection of contributions from theatreworkers and critics.

Hauptfleisch, Temple, *Theatre and Society in South Africa: Reflections in a Fractured Mirror* (Pretoria: J. L. van Schaik, 1997). Survey from a broadly culturalist perspective.

Kershaw, Baz, *The Radical in Performance Between Brecht and Baudrillard* (London: Routledge, 1999). Gloomy analysis of political impact of 'Western' theatre between modernism and postmodernism.

Spivak, Gayatri Chakravorty, 'Can the Subaltern Speak? Speculations on Widow Sacrifice' (1985), repr. in P. Williams and L. Chrisman (eds.), *Colonial Discourse and Post-Colonial Theory: A Reader* (Hemel Hempstead: Harvester Wheatsheaf, 1993), 66–111. A seminal essay on the issue of 'voicing' the politically voiceless.

Thompson, Leonard, *A History of South Africa*, rev. edn. (New Haven: Yale University Press, 1995). Concise and admirably objective account.

Index

115

Recent and Forthcoming Titles in the New Series of

WRITERS AND THEIR WORK

RECENT & FORTHCOMING TITLES

Title	Author
Ivor Gurney	John Lucas
Hamlet 2/e	Ann Thompson & Neil Taylor
Thomas Hardy	Peter Widdowson
Tony Harrison	Joe Kelleher
William Hazlitt	J. B. Priestley; R. L. Brett (intro. by Michael Foot)
Seamus Heaney 2/e	Andrew Murphy
George Herbert	T.S. Eliot (intro. by Peter Porter)
Geoffrey Hill	Andrew Roberts
Gerard Manley Hopkins	Daniel Brown
Henrik Ibsen	Sally Ledger
Kazuo Ishiguro	Cynthia Wong
Henry James – The Later Writing	Barbara Hardy
James Joyce	Steven Connor
Julius Caesar	Mary Hamer
Franz Kafka	Michael Wood
John Keats	Kelvin Everest
Hanif Kureishi	Ruvani Ranasinha
Samuel Johnson	Liz Bellamy
William Langland. Piers Plowman	Claire Marshall
King Lear	Terence Hawkes
Philip Larkin	Laurence Lerner
D. H. Lawrence	Linda Ruth Williams
Doris Lessing	Elizabeth Maslen
C. S. Lewis	William Gray
Wyndham Lewis and Modernism	Andrzej Gasiorek
David Lodge	Bernard Bergonzi
Katherine Mansfield	Andrew Bennett
Christopher Marlowe	Thomas Healy
Andrew Marvell	Annabel Patterson
Ian McEwan	Kiernan Ryan
Measure for Measure	Kate Chedgzoy
Merchant of Venice	Warren Chernaik
A Midsummer Night's Dream	Helen Hackett
Alice Munro	Ailsa Cox
Vladimir Nabokov	Neil Cornwell
V. S. Naipaul	Suman Gupta
Edna O'Brien	Amanda Greenwood
Flann O'Brien	Joe Brooker
Ben Okri	Robert Fraser
George Orwell	Douglas Kerr
Walter Pater	Laurel Brake
Brian Patten	Linda Cookson
Caryl Phillips	Helen Thomas
Harold Pinter	Mark Batty
Sylvia Plath 2/e	Elisabeth Bronfen
Jean Rhys	Helen Carr
Richard II	Margaret Healy
Richard III	Edward Burns
Dorothy Richardson	Carol Watts
John Wilmot, Earl of Rochester	Germaine Greer
Romeo and Juliet	Sasha Roberts
Christina Rossetti	Kathryn Burlinson
Salman Rushdie	Damian Grant

RECENT & FORTHCOMING TITLES

TITLES IN PREPARATION

Title	Author
Chinua Achebe	*Nahem Yousaf*
Ama Ata Aidoo	*Nana Wilson-Tagoe*
Matthew Arnold	*Kate Campbell*
Margaret Atwood	*Marion Wynne-Davies*
Jane Austen	*Robert Miles*
John Banville	*Peter Dempsey*
Pat Barker	*Sharon Monteith*
Julian Barnes	*Matthew Pateman*
Samuel Beckett	*Keir Elam*
William Blake	*Steven Vine*
Elizabeth Bowen	*Maud Ellmann*
Charlotte Brontë	*Patsy Stoneman*
Robert Browning	*John Woodford*
John Bunyan	*Tamsin Spargoe*
Cymbeline	*Peter Swaab*
Daniel Defoe	*Jim Rigney*
Anita Desai	*Elaine Ho*
Shashi Deshpande	*Amrita Bhalla*
Margaret Drabble	*Glenda Leeming*
John Dryden	*David Hopkins*
T. S. Eliot	*Colin MacCabe*
J. G. Farrell	*John McLeod*
John Fowles	*William Stephenson*
Brian Friel	*Geraldine Higgins*
Athol Fugard	*Dennis Walder*
Nadine Gordimer	*Lewis Nkosi*
Geoffrey Grigson	*R. M. Healey*
Neil Gunn	*J. B. Pick*
Geoffrey Hill	*Andrew Roberts*
Gerard Manley Hopkins	*Daniel Brown*
Ted Hughes	*Susan Bassnett*
Samuel Johnson	*Liz Dellamy*
Ben Jonson	*Anthony Johnson*
John Keats	*Kelvin Everest*
James Kelman	*Gustav Klaus*
Rudyard Kipling	*Jan Montefiore*
Charles and Mary Lamb	*Michael Baron*
Wyndham Lewis	*Andrzej Gasiorak*
Malcolm Lowry	*Hugh Stevens*
Macbeth	*Kate McCluskie*
Katherine Mansfield	*Andrew Bennett*
Una Marson & Louise Bennett	*Alison Donnell*
Merchant of Venice	*Warren Chernaik*
John Milton	*Jonathan Sawday*
Bharati Mukherjee	*Manju Sampat*
Alice Munro	*Ailsa Cox*
R. K. Narayan	*Shirley Chew*
New Women Novelists of the Late 19th Century	*Gail Cunningham*
Grace Nichols	*Sarah Lawson-Welsh*
Edna O'Brien	*Amanda Greenwood*
Ben Okri	*Robert Fraser*
Caryl Phillips	*Helen Thomas*

TITLES IN PREPARATION

Title	Author
Religious Poets of the 17th Century	Helen Wilcox
Revenge Tragedy	Janet Clare
Samuel Richardson	David Deeming
Nayantara Sahgal	Ranjana Ash
Sam Selvon	
Sir Walter Scott	Harriet Harvey-Wood
Mary Shelley	Catherine Sharrock
Charlotte Smith & Helen Williams	Angela Keane
Stevie Smith	Martin Gray
R. L. Stevenson	David Robb
Gertrude Stein	Nicola Shaughnessy
Bram Stoker	Andrew Maunder
Tom Stoppard	Nicholas Cadden
Jonathan Swift	Ian Higgins
Algernon Swinburne	Catherine Maxwell
The Tempest	Gordon McMullan
Tennyson	Seamus Perry
W. M. Thackeray	Richard Salmon
Three Avant-Garde Poets	Peter Middleton
Derek Walcott	Stephen Regan
Marina Warner	Laurence Coupe
Jeanette Winterson	Margaret Reynolds
Women Romantic Poets	Anne Janowitz
Women Writers of the 17th Century	Ramona Wray
Women Writers at the Fin de Siècle	Angelique Richardson